LAUGHTER ON WHEELS
A Century of Motoring Humour

STONE CRACKER JOHN
"The rich go by in their wildcat machinery and they kicks up the dust and they spoils all the greenery"

Popular ballad of the 1900s

THE AUTHORS

For nearly 40 years John Bullock and Bob Sicot were two of the top PR men in Europe, working at the 'sharp end' of the international scene and directing their companies' public relations activities. John Bullock left Fleet Street to work for the car makers Rootes and Chrysler, and Robert Sicot performed a similar function for Simca, Renault and Ford of Europe. They also acted as PR consultants to several other leading international motor companies and motoring organizations.

As friends and rivals during a highly competitive period in the development of the motor car, they have always had two things in common – a great sense of humour and an uncanny ability to become involved in many of the hilarious episodes which took place in a motoring world full of entertaining characters and events.

John Bullock has been a prolific writer for much of his life, while Bob Sicot's talent with a pen and sketch pad has also become well-known. It is his cartoons which illustrate many of the stories recorded at random by John Bullock in this refreshingly lighthearted book about the motor industry's first hundred years.

Both men have been honoured by the Guild of Motoring Writers for the part they played during their time in the motor industry.

LAUGHTER ON WHEELS
A Century of Motoring Humour

JOHN BULLOCK & BOB SICOT

MRP

MOTOR RACING PUBLICATIONS LTD
Unit 6, The Pilton Estate, 46 Pitlake, Croydon CRO 3RY, England

First published 1995

British Library Cataloguing in Publication Data
Bullock, John
Laughter on Wheels: A Century of Motoring
Humour
I. Title II. Sicot, Bob
796.70207
ISBN 1-899870-03-2

Photoset by JDB Typesetting, Croydon
Printed in Great Britain by
Hartnolls Limited, Bodmin, Cornwall

CONTENTS

INTRODUCTION

Laughter on Wheels is a topical tribute to a centenary of motoring and an entertaining account of the car makers, the models they produced and the men and women who made them famous – or sometimes infamous! The events have been recorded by two men well qualified to know what has been going on behind the scenes in an industry which has been in the headlines since the first motor car chugged its way into people's lives.

The stories include many personal recollections of the postwar era by John Bullock and Robert Sicot and some of their friends and colleagues from rival motor companies, who have delved into their past to produce one of the most entertaining accounts yet written about motor cars and motoring people.

The book is also a random account of some of the more hilarious events which have taken place during the development of the motor car, from the days when motoring was only for the very rich, to the present time when it has become an essential part of everyday life.

Acknowledgements

The authors are grateful for the help they have received from friends and former colleagues and particularly from Harry Calton, who spent many years with the Ford Motor Company and as Head of Product Information was involved with many important new model launches and other major events. He is now the Director of Public Affairs for Aston Martin.

SNAKES AND BAGPIPES

International rallies used to provide a welcome opportunity for some of Europe's top racing drivers to enjoy themselves, earn some additional cash and do something different. Stirling Moss, Mike Hawthorn, Peter Collins, Ivor Bueb, Jack Fairman, Leslie Johnson, Les Leston, Peter Jopp and Ken Wharton were all regular members of the Rootes works teams and combined rally driving with Grand Prix and sportscar racing.

Apart from being an outstanding driver, Ken Wharton was also a brilliant engineer, which became very evident when he took part in driving trials, became the trials champion and proved to be almost unbeatable at the wheel of one of the many specials he built himself. I competed against him on several occasions, in trials and rallies, and he was always fun to be with because although he had a strong desire to win, he never lost his keen sense of humour.

He was popular with everyone, except on one occasion, when a jealous husband suspected, quite rightly, that Ken was having an affair with his rather pretty blonde wife. She was a member of one of the women's teams in that year's Monte Carlo Rally and to try to get the evidence he wanted, her husband employed a Birmingham private detective to follow them to Monte Carlo. However, it was wishful thinking on his part to hope to outwit Ken in that way. Even an experienced rally driver would have had difficulty in keeping up with him once the rally commenced. A private detective driving a prewar Wolseley and without any experience of the conditions he would have to face, just wasn't up to the task.

His problems began on their way to the start: Ken and some of the other competitors, including the blonde, decided to spend a night in Paris. After dinner they all went off to a nightclub in the *Rue Pigalle*, closely followed by the private detective. As the lights dimmed for the cabaret the private eye saw his opportunity, and while everyone's attention was fixed on the Swedish 'exotic dancer', who was using a rather large snake in her act, he crawled on hands and knees between the tables with his camera, to try to take an incriminating photograph of Ken and the blonde with their arms round each other.

Flashbulbs let off unexpectedly in a Paris night club can have a startling effect on French businessmen, particularly those whose wives are under the impression that they are away on a business trip. They can have an even greater effect on a snake, and while several members of the audience screamed and climbed onto chairs, it took its chance for freedom.

Pandemonium broke out as it slithered its way across the floor and out through the door, hotly pursued by the scantily dressed dancer. The manager of the nightclub, aided by a rather evil-looking doorman, grabbed the private detective as he tried to escape and held him until several *gendarmes* arrived to add to his misery. The private eye eventually handed over the film, along with the several thousand extra francs which had been added to his bill to pay for the damage he had caused, including the loss of the snake.

The private eye arrived back at his hotel with an empty wallet, probably a wiser, but certainly a very much poorer man, with no means of settling his bill the next morning. Credit cards were unheard of and he was forced to stay in Paris until more money could be sent from England. By the time he was able to settle his hotel bill and leave, Ken and the blonde, along with all the other competitors, were well on their way to Monte Carlo.

The rally was over and the last party had ended before his Wolseley was seen chugging down the hill into Monte Carlo. By its appearance it had

obviously been in contact with several hazards along the way and Ken couldn't resist offering him a lift back to England "in case you get into any further mischief".

It was difficult not to feel rather sorry for the man, but there is a great bond of friendship between rally drivers and he had taken on an almost impossible assignment, with little chance of getting the evidence he was after.

Sadly, Ken Wharton was later killed in a race in New Zealand and the very pretty blonde with the jealous husband was sent to prison for procuring an abortion.

Ivor Bueb was another talented racing driver who was always good company on a rally. After he had won the Le Mans 24-Hours race for the second time, I did a deal with him which ensured that the Rootes team always had plenty of francs when we were abroad and while foreign currency was in such short supply. Ivor's prize money was of little use to him anywhere other than in France, because he was unable to take his winnings out of the country. We agreed a rate of exchange which enabled me to make use of some of his prize money and I paid him the equivalent in Sterling when we returned to England.

He was a member of the Rootes rally team on several occasions and his staple diet during a rally was baked beans. Before the start he stuffed cans of them in every available space in the car and whenever he felt a bit peckish would eat them cold straight from the tin. I drove his car at the end of one event and thought something must have happened to the transmission until I traced the noise to the scores of empty baked bean cans rattling about in the back.

Whenever our team did well in the Monte, Lord Rootes' younger son Brian flew out to help us celebrate. Ivor's francs always came in handy at the casino and although Ivor never played the tables, he'd have an occasional flutter on the one-arm bandits round the walls of the bar. He took on a bet one evening that he could run round the room putting money in every machine and get back to the bar before they had stopped spinning. With other competitors and some of the British journalists acting as marshals, the circuit was cleared and Ivor set off. He lost his bet, but hit the jackpot with two of the one-arm bandits, providing enough francs for a party for all the British competitors.

For someone with more francs than he knew what to do with, winning one, let alone two jackpots the same evening, just didn't seem possible, but none of us complained. The party went on until dawn and we all returned to our hotel in high spirits. Competitors who had already gone to bed and put their shoes outside their doors to be cleaned had a shock the next morning when they found that some of the more inebriated revellers had put their shoes in the water buckets placed along the corridors in case of fire.

It was even more of a shock to Brian when he woke up to find that one of the pairs belonged to his wife Bet, who had gone to bed early after having dinner with some friends. Brian came knocking on my door at some unearthly hour, wanting to know if I had enough francs left for him to take Bet shopping for some new shoes. Despite Ivor's two jackpots, it proved to be a rather expensive evening after all.

The Rootes team always stayed at the Metropole Hotel, which was a favourite with most of the competitors and has a really magnificent staircase. The Army entered a team one year led by Major Donald MacLeod. As soon as they reached Monte Carlo the fun started and they lost no time in joining in all the usual end-of-rally celebrations. Peter Dimmock was driving one of our cars and planned to go skiing in Austria on his way home. He had persuaded Norman Garrad, the Rootes Competitions Manager, to allow his skis be taken to Monte Carlo in the team transporter.

Unfortunately for Peter, Donald MacLeod found them and after a particularly good evening at the Tip Top Club, decided to use them to ski down the staircase of the Metropole Hotel. We were coming through the swing doors into the foyer just as he had reached the point of no return. Peter's cries were too late and a few seconds later skier and skis landed at the bottom of the stairs in a heap. Had Donald been sober he would probably have broken a leg, or worse, but fortunately only the skis were damaged. The management didn't take kindly to their magnificent staircase being used as a ski slope, but as there hadn't been any damage done to the hotel and none of the guests complained, they were persuaded to forget the incident.

However, the manager of the casino was not so forgiving the following evening when Donald and his fellow officers were probably the first and last people to bring play to a halt in the famous *Salle Privee*. Immaculate in full dress uniform and kilts, they smuggled some bagpipes into an ante-room and at the stroke of midnight orders rang out and all three slow-marched through the room, with Donald leading the way playing *Scotland the Brave* on the pipes.

Play stopped at all the tables and everyone stood and clapped until the last strains had died away as the piper and his two escorts slow-marched out of the casino. As they left they were handed their passports by the manager and told not to darken the casino's portals again.

The Monte Carlo Rally doesn't seem to be the same any more. Perhaps it's just as well.

THE MONTE CARLO CHALLENGE

Since it was first run in the Twenties, the Monte Carlo Rally has been the ultimate challenge for cars and their crews to contend with the worst winter road and weather conditions in Europe and reach Monaco on time and in one piece.

Although the Rootes Group employed some of Britain's finest Grand Prix drivers and won every other major international rally after the war, a Rootes car only won the Monte outright on one occasion. That was in 1955, when a privately entered Sunbeam-Talbot driven by two Norwegian businessmen beat the cream of all the works teams.

Captain Per Malling and Gunnar Fadum were experienced competitors, but few people gave them much chance of winning, as strong teams had been entered by every major manufacturer in Europe. Although their victory was unexpected, it was still an important success for Rootes, because it proved the reliability and ruggedness of the new Sunbeam-Talbot. We made arrangements for their winning car to be flown back to London with Per Malling and Gunnar Fadum as soon as the result had been confirmed, so that it could go on show at the Rootes headquarters in Piccadilly while the rally was still in the news and fresh in everyone's mind.

Although the Rootes factory team had won seven major awards that year, including the manufacturer's team prize and the *Coupe des Dames* for the first woman driver, it was the winning car that the public wanted to see, and particularly the condition it was in after tackling the ice, snow, rain and mud on the 2,000-mile drive to Monte Carlo.

The two Norwegians and their Sunbeam-Talbot went on board a Bristol Freighter belonging to Silver City Airways for the flight to London and when the plane landed, Per Malling and Gunnar Fadum were whisked off to a hotel to get some badly needed sleep before the following day's press reception at Devonshire House. Their car was taken to the main Rootes service station at Ladbroke Hall for safe keeping. As there was so little time in which to get everything ready, a promotions team worked throughout the night at Devonshire House, preparing a special display which would have the Norwegians' car as the centrepiece.

Fortunately, everything was finished on time, but my colleagues and I had a shock when the winning Sunbeam-Talbot was delivered to the showroom. The over-zealous service manager at Ladbroke Hall, on learning that it was to go on show, had arranged for another team to work throughout the night cleaning off all the grime and mud and giving a high gloss finish to the bodywork and chrome. By the time they had finished, apart from the rally plates, there was nothing to show that it had just taken part in Europe's most gruelling rally and little to distinguish it from any other used car in the showrooms.

We had to get some mud back on the car as quickly as possible and my neighbour in Surrey agreed to let us drive it round one of the muddiest fields on his farm until it looked more like a rally car. When it was put on the plinth in the Rootes Devonshire House showrooms later that morning, it did at least look the part and nobody was any the wiser.

Before the Sunbeam-Talbot was shipped back to Norway later that week I arranged for some of the motoring writers to drive it for a few hours and report on its condition and performance. One of them was the fun-loving John Bolster, a racing driver turned journalist and television commentator, who wrote for *Autosport*. He collected the car from Devonshire House and after driving round London for an hour or so, parked it in Park Lane while he went to lunch with some friends at the Steering Wheel Club in nearby Brick Street.

When he returned an hour or two later, he found two very irate London bobbies making arrangements to have it taken away. When he realized that the winning car still had its foreign number plates and was sporting a Norwegian flag, John walked up to the two policemen and, pointing to the car, repeated the words of a Norwegian drinking song he had learned during one of his visits to Scandinavia. Every time they asked to see his driving licence, he repeated the words of the song and added a few phrases of his own for good measure.

It didn't take long for the two policemen to realize that they weren't getting anywhere with the tall, handlebar-moustached madman with a deer stalker hat and gave up the attempt to make him understand. He told me later that as they wandered off, one turned to the other and said, "Bloody foreigners. London's full of them."

TUBELESS TYRES AND
VIVE LE SPORT

When tubeless tyres first arrived on the British market, the Dunlop company persuaded Norman Garrad, the Rootes Competitions Manager, to fit them to the works Sunbeam-Talbots in that year's Monte Carlo Rally. Unfortunately, this proved to be a big mistake because the tyres at that time couldn't stand up to the buffeting the cars received in the mountains on some of the toughest sections of the route. Every time a wheel-rim became damaged through striking a kerb or some other obstruction, the tyre lost pressure.

Norman became very concerned that they would let us down when the leading 100 cars took part in the speed test over the mountain circuit above Monte Carlo on the final day. The answer seemed to be to fit inner tubes as soon as the team arrived in Monte Carlo, but we needed to make the change at a garage outside the town and away from prying eyes. Finding a suitable one which had enough of the right size tubes, and was willing to fit them quickly so that the cars wouldn't be late arriving at the finish and lose valuable points, shouldn't have been too much of a problem – or so we thought – and after taking a look at the mountain circuit the drivers would be tackling the following day, Norman and I decided to have lunch at a delightful little *auberge* overlooking the town.

We agreed that while he drove on into Monte Carlo to check on the team's progress after lunch, I would stay and telephone some garages until I found one who would do the job for us. I went steadily through the list of them in the local telephone directory and tried to tell the owners what we needed, but as soon as I explained that our cars were running on tyres without inner tubes, they obviously thought they were dealing with some drunken Englishman and hung up.

It was late afternoon before I eventually found a garage proprietor who didn't think I was completely mad and agreed to fit the inner tubes for us. Relieved that I had at last succeeded in finding a suitable garage I ordered a cognac from the owner of the *auberge*, who must have overheard my heated exchanges with the garage men, and also asked to have a brochure in case I wanted to bring my family to stay there later. As I glanced at the brochure, I noticed that the staff were fluent in several foreign languages, including English.

"Who speaks English?" I asked the owner.

"I do," he replied.

I gave him a look which I hoped summed up my feelings adequately and said:

"Why didn't you tell me that before? I could have done with your help in trying to explain about tubeless tyres."

He shrugged his shoulders:

"I don't think I would have been of much help. I couldn't understand what you were talking about either. Whoever heard of tyres without inner tubes?"

Fortunately, everything went according to plan and our team cars got their inner tubes before the start of the mountain circuit. The following day Norman Garrad and I found a good vantage spot overlooking Monte Carlo where we could watch the final speed trial taking place in the mountains. The route had been closed to other traffic for the day, because 100 cars travelling flat-out in the same direction can be dangerous enough, without having to miss vehicles coming in the other direction, but that year something must have gone wrong.

As the first cars came roaring up the mountain, round the corner just above us came one of the French 2CV Citroens – affectionately known as tin snails

or racing dustbins – driven by a rather large Frenchman wearing a beret, and filled with adults and children clutching *baguettes*. They seemed oblivious to the danger they were in and waved happily to the spectators lining the route as their little Citroen sped down the mountain with its driver refusing to stop or give way. One after another the competitors coming up the mountain had to take evasive action and we learned later that although there were a number of near misses, fortunately nobody was hurt. It could only have happened in France: "*Vive le sport*".

IN THE SOUP

Tubeless tyres were not the only innovation to undergo experimentation during the Monte Carlo Rally. When Heinz decided to sell cans of self-heating soup, someone must have suggested to their marketing men that they could get a lot of topical publicity by persuading competitors on the rally to take cans of their new soup with them. They had, however, overlooked the fact that every inch of space in a rally car is needed for carrying spares and other essential equipment, like shovels. Boxes of self-heating soup would come low down on any competitor's list of priorities.

The Heinz man who was sent to Paris, one of the main starting points for the rally that year, soon realized this and, despite all his efforts, the supply of self-heating soup was still intact when he made his way to the ever-popular Fred Payne's bar – no doubt to drown his sorrows and enjoy his last evening in Paris before returning home.

Fred Payne was an Englishman whose famous bar was always a focal point for competitors and motoring enthusiasts. He'd gone to Paris in the Thirties and made it his home. As soon as the war was over his bar was back in business and my colleagues and I made a point of seeing him when we were in the capital. Fred seemed to know everybody: whether any friends were in town; where they were staying and if they were likely to be paying him a visit. Messages left with him for other competitors usually reached them. It was a quite remarkable place and Fred was a very remarkable man.

The year of the self-heating soup we had loaned the BBC a large Humber, so that Peter Dimmock, who was then the anchor man on the BBC's popular *Sportsview* programme, and his team could cover the rally and give their reports added interest by being able to describe their own experiences as competitors. The programme's Editor was Paul Fox, who went on to be Head of BBC and Yorkshire Television and receive a knighthood. He also became Chairman of the Racecourse Owners Association and a member of the British Horseracing Board. Peter Dimmock, later Head of BBC Outside Broadcasts, was a keen driver and we all admired his enthusiasm and professionalism whenever he took part in a rally.

The Humber was not really an ideal rally car, but the BBC team needed a vehicle capable of carrying all their equipment and which would still enable them to meet their daily transmission schedules and get to Monte Carlo in time to film the finish. The irrepressible Ronnie Noble was a regular member of the *Sportsview* Monte Carlo team, but he looked upon the rally as an opportunity to have some fun as well as provide BBC coverage. He knew their chances of winning were slim and consequently didn't share Peter's determination to try to finish as high up the list as possible. Neither did he agree with his insistence that the BBC team should retire to bed early on the evening before the start. When Ronnie was sure that Peter and the others were in bed, he crept out of their hotel and headed for some Paris nightlife and Fred Payne's bar, where we had agreed to meet.

The man from Heinz, who was also there, cheered up when Ronnie arrived and obviously thought that he may have one last chance of turning failure into success if he managed to get some of the self-heating soup on board the BBC Humber. After several glasses of champagne Ronnie didn't need much persuading that the soup would be of more use during the rally than the shovels and other equipment, particularly as he had no intention of digging the Humber out of any ditch if it did go off the road: some hot soup while they waited for help to arrive seemed a far more sensible proposition. So, by the time the BBC Humber set off for Monte Carlo, Ronnie had made sure that there were several cases of self-heating soup in the boot.

Road and weather conditions deteriorated rapidly after the competitors left Paris and they were soon battling against ice and snow. The BBC Humber was one of the first cars to hit black ice and spin off the road, coming to rest only a few feet from a hedge. When Peter Dimmock opened the boot and found boxes of soup instead of the mats and shovels they needed, according to Ronnie, he nearly went berserk.

Something would have to be done to get the car back onto the road as quickly as possible, or they would lose any chance they had of doing some filming and making their next programme transmission on time. If that happened Ronnie would be in serious trouble. The thought struck him that it might be possible to use the hot soup to melt the ice on the tyre tracks left by the car as it skidded off the road. They might then be able to get the

Humber back onto the road by keeping the wheels on the melted tracks and hopefully getting enough grip to propel the car backwards.

The idea seemed worth trying and Ronnie began opening up the cans and pouring their hot contents onto the ice. To his surprise the ice did start to melt as more hot soup was poured along the tracks. He was still putting down the contents of the last few cans when, without warning, Peter jumped into the Humber, pressed the starter, selected reverse gear and revved the engine. The rear wheels began to spin, throwing up a steady stream of melted ice and soup, and Ronnie was soon covered in a colourful, but sticky mixture of wet ice and some of Heinz's 57 different varieties.

It was hardly surprising that the man from Heinz didn't get the reply he was expecting when he telephoned Ronnie after the rally to find out what he thought about their new soup!

THE WEYBRIDGE BOWL

Although the last motor race took place there in 1939, on a hot and sunny August Bank Holiday Monday before a large crowd of spectators, Brooklands is still remembered as the place which, more than any other, caught the imagination of the public and was responsible for many important developments in the British motor industry. It was more than just a race track, and after being opened in June 1907 as Britain's first custom-built racing circuit, it soon became established as a centre of motoring excellence and technical achievement. To many it remains a shrine to those men and women of courage, who enjoyed living their lives in the fast track and whose exploits made them famous.

It was built to be the world's first banked motor racing circuit, and make Britain the centre of the motoring scene, by the husband and wife team of Hugh and Ethel Locke King. They set aside some farmland beside the river Wey, felled hundreds of trees, levelled the ground and built a road round the site. The cost alone of laying the track, building three bridges and erecting more than eight miles of fencing, was said to have been in the region of £22,000.

Up to 2,000 men were employed throughout the winter, many of them camping on the site. Lots of farm buildings were demolished, the River Wey was diverted in two places and seven miles of railway lines were laid over the estate to bring in the 200,000 tons of gravel and cement needed to build the famous banking.

The magnitude of the task nearly bankrupted Hugh Locke King and the strain seriously affected his health. In the end it was his wife Ethel, with the help of her family, who took over responsibility for getting the track completed to the design of Colonel Holden of the Royal Engineers.

At the opening ceremony she led the way round the circuit in her Itala car, followed by Lord Lonsdale, of Lonsdale belt fame, who was the President of the Brooklands Automobile Racing Club, and the Vice-President, Lord Montagu of Beaulieu, the first man to drive a motor car into the House of Commons forecourt, and members of the committee. As was typical of the time, the Club's committee had been stacked with members of the aristocracy, who included the Duke of Westminster, Viscount Churchill, the Earl of Sefton, the Duke of Beaufort, the Earl of Dudley, Lord Northcliffe,

Lord Tollemache and Prince Francis of Teck.

At the opening there were also demonstration laps by various drivers, including a particularly exciting one by Charles Jarrott in his big Napier, perhaps a foretaste of the shape of things to come.

With the first race meeting set for July 6, the racing driver S F Edge decided to steal most of the limelight by booking the circuit on June 28 for an attempt to set a single-handed, 24-hour record in his 60hp Napier. He thundered round the track at an average speed of 65.9mph, accompanied by Blackburn, his racing mechanic, and refreshed himself with cocoa, beef tea, bananas and grapes while the car was being refuelled.

Excitement grew as the 18th hour approached, not because of the distance covered, the car's outstanding performance or the fact that the track was being lit at night by hundreds of flares and red lanterns, but because medical experts had predicted that the strain of driving virtually non-stop for that length of time would cause the driver to go mad.

There was almost a sense of anti-climax among some of the more ghoulish members of the public when it didn't happen and Edge continued lapping the circuit at high speed, stopping occasionally to refuel the car and himself, until by the time the 24 hours was up, the Napier had covered 1,582 miles and he and his mechanic seemed none the worse for their exertions.

There were complaints of cheating during the races on the first day. Charles Jarrott revealed that some competitors had been feeding pure oxygen into their car's carburettors from cylinders they were carrying with them during the race, which he said was on a par with being caught doping horses, and insisted that the practice should be stamped out without delay. There was obviously skullduggery afoot on the motor racing circuits even then....

Brooklands quickly became an integral part of Britain's motoring scene, but it also developed into an important aviation centre when Sir Alliott Verdon-Roe built his first Avro aeroplane in a shed at the foot of the test hill and flew it on June 28, 1908, to record the first flight by an Englishman in an English-built aircraft.

The Royal Flying Corps and the Royal Air Force moved into Brooklands with the outbreak of the First World War and Bleriot, Sopwith and Vickers all built aircraft there. Extensive repairs were necessary before the circuit could be reopened for motor racing in May 1920.

Brooklands developed into more than just an important race track and a centre for aviation. It also became an influential test circuit, where motor manufacturers launched and demonstrated their new models, and was a constant hive of activity, with motoring journalists looking for hot tips and 'scoops', rather like racing tipsters on Newmarket Heath. On race days there were bookmakers, like the famous Long Tom, ready to offer the public odds on their favourite racing drivers and their cars.

The *Autocar* became the first British motoring magazine when it was launched on November 2, 1895. That was also the year when the pioneer motorist Sir David Salomons predicted that the motor car would revolutionize travel throughout the world and that the time would arrive when England would become one of the chief centres of the motor industry – brave words indeed as it was not until a year later that the first Daimler was built in Coventry and Britain's motor industry was born. A man with a red flag still had to walk 20 yards ahead of every motor vehicle to warn other road users of the danger, and the British Government was enforcing a strict 4mph speed limit.

To emphasize his faith in the future of the motor car, however, Sir David had organized the country's first motor show on October 15, 1895, at the Agricultural Showground, Tunbridge Wells, Kent. All the cars on display had been imported and the show was only open for two hours in the afternoon, from three o'clock until five, but it was very well attended. The first London motor show was held the following year, when H J Lawson organized one at the Imperial Institute in South Kensington. The Prince of Wales went along and pressure was brought to bear on the Government to do away with the need for a man with a red flag and to raise the speed limit to 12mph.

This was marked by an Emancipation Run from London to Brighton, which the Veteran Car Club still celebrates each year. There were 56 entries for that first Brighton Run in 1896 and 13 reached Brighton, an indication of the determination and spirit of those pioneer motorists, but also the unreliability of some of their cars.

The *Autocar* also created another first in the early Twenties when the magazine invented the road test. The publisher realized that standard criteria were needed so that uniform comparisons could be made of every car's acceleration, maximum speed, braking performance, fuel consumption and roadholding, as well as its overall quality and interior dimensions.

Brooklands provided by far the best facilities for performance testing and the magazine arranged with the track's owners to have the full use of the circuit throughout the year, even during the winter months, when it was closed to the public for maintenance and general repairs.

Several times a week the *Autocar* test team made the journey to Weybridge from the magazine's offices at Waterloo. On arrival at the circuit each new model was weighed on the weighbridge adjoining the club house, and ballast was added if the member of staff doing the testing that day was below a certain weight, to ensure that each car carried the same weight of driver and the same number and weight of passengers.

A measured mile had been permanently marked on the circuit and the test team used a variety of stopwatches. It was before the days of a fifth wheel and perhaps rather primitive compared with the modern hi-tech equipment like the electronic Correvit beam in use now, but it worked and produced the results the public wanted to read about.

The banked track was used for achieving maximum speed figures, the finishing straight for braking and acceleration tests, and the one-in-five test hill for revealing a car's hill-climbing ability and torque.

By the Thirties the magazine was road-testing in the region of 70 cars a year and continued to do so. After the Second World War motor manufacturers ensured that the *Autocar* and *Motor* magazines always had the first of their new production models to road-test and photograph some weeks ahead of the launch date, so that full reports could be published to coincide with the announcement and the independent performance figures the magazines achieved could be used in the company's advertising.

The magazines always maintained strict secrecy and there were very few occasions when details or photographs of any new models were published while the cars were in their hands. There was one occasion, however, when a new Sunbeam was being tested by Peter Garnier, the *Autocar*'s Sports Editor and a very experienced rally driver. As luck would have it, he lost control of the Sunbeam on a bend at the end of a long straight. The car ran up a bank and slid along the front wall of a row of cottages, coming to rest finely balanced across the front gates of two of them. The elderly occupants must have had a shock when they heard the sound of expensive metalwork tearing along a stone wall, and looked out of their window to see a brand-new car perched only a few feet away. They were also trapped in the front gardens of their cottages until a breakdown vehicle with a crane arrived to lift the Sunbeam clear. There was nothing Rootes or the magazine could do to prevent photographs being taken of the new model, and it was bad luck on Peter Garnier, who was trying to get the best possible performance figures at the time.

The magazine's Editor, Maurice Smith, who was also an experienced motorist and test driver, had the misfortune to lose control of a new Aston Martin – a marque which he himself owned – at Silverstone when he was trying to get the top speed figure being claimed by the manufacturer. The car spun several times before shooting backwards and becoming embedded in a bank. It needed a tow truck to get it out, but fortunately it wasn't damaged beyond repair. Perhaps it was lucky for everyone concerned that it was the Editor who had dropped the clanger on that occasion and not one of the *Autocar* staff!

Bill Boddy, the former Editor of *Motor Sport* magazine, described the Surrey track as "the most desirable place on this earth" in his foreword to

Brooklands: a Pictorial History. Few of those who, like I did as a boy, spent many weekends there before the war watching the greats in action, would disagree. There was always so much going on at one of the track's three circuits. A special one, known as the Campbell Circuit, was used for the great man to show off his famous Bluebird, which was often housed in the Thomson and Taylor's shed in the Brooklands paddock and wheeled out on special occasions. The team of designers and mechanics at Thomson and Taylor were involved in speed record cars for more than 20 years.

Malcolm Campbell took the Land Speed Record a remarkable nine times between 1922 and 1935, when he reached an astonishing 301.13mph. Brooklands was closely involved with four of those records and the wind tunnel there was used for testing the car's shape and wind resistance. The body of the 1935 car was made in the Campbell Shed at the track.

To the delight of the crowd, his latest record breaker would be wheeled out onto the circuit and Malcolm Campbell would trundle his Bluebird round the course while everyone cheered and felt a pride in British achievement. Racing also took place on most weekends during the summer months on either the Mountain Circuit or the Outer Circuit.

When Brooklands was opened in 1907 the Land Speed Record stood at under 130mph. Forty years later, a Brooklands-built car took it to nearly 400mph, when the Railton used by John Cobb set a new record of 394.20mph and actually exceeded 400mph on one run.

For several years Land Speed Records were broken at Brooklands, until more room was required. The last time was in 1922 when Kenelm Lee Guinness, of KLG sparking plug fame, achieved 135.75mph in the 350hp Sunbeam, which then became the first of Malcolm Campbell's record-breaking Bluebirds.

There was even a Brooklands connection with Land Speed Record attempts in 1995 when Richard Noble chose it as the nostalgic venue for his announcement that Thrust SCC, the latest Land Speed Record contender, would be driven by Andy Green.

Although it had been the scene of several tragedies, Brooklands was always a place of enjoyment and laughter, where the drivers and spectators expected to have a good time. There was certainly plenty of laughter there on August 7, 1939, but few people could have realized that they were attending the last ever meeting at the famous track.

For months the newspapers and the radio had been full of foreboding and war began to seem inevitable. Even the summer weather had been wet and miserable, but on the morning of the final race meeting all that changed. The circuit was bathed in glorious sunshine and as a steady stream of cars poured into the paddock and car park, everybody seemed to forget the events of the previous weeks and looked forward to some top-class entertainment. They were not to be disappointed. Even the new cocktail bar in the Clubhouse had been equipped with the very latest in beer engines, so that the pints could flow fast and furious to satisfy those with even the most insatiable of thirsts.

The racing also provided top-class entertainment. Raymond Mays in his ERA beat Prince Bira's Maserati to win the main event and take the Campbell Trophy. The popular band leader Billy Cotton won another race in his ERA, and the bespectacled Bob Gerard, along with Percy Maclure and Wilkie Wilkinson, all won races in their Rileys.

The impressive works V12 Lagondas, driven by Charles Brackenbury and Lord Selsdon, who had been third and fourth at Le Mans two weeks earlier, roared over the finishing line to take the first two places in their race, with 'Brack' putting in the fastest lap average of 127.7mph. A burly man, with a large moustache, he drove bareheaded wearing an old sleeveless sweater.

There was a special cheer when Dorothy Stanley-Turner won in her supercharged MG Midget. She was a very pretty member of the 'powder puff and lipstick brigade', the group of women drivers who showed tremendous courage and ability on the track and were always very difficult to beat, but who carried a powder puff and lipstick with them in the cockpit of their cars so that, even when they had just finished a gruelling race, they always faced the cameras' cars looking their best. She put her victory down

to the lucky white elephant mascot which an admirer had given her just before the race.

As the shadows began to lengthen, G L Baker made a piece of last-minute motoring history when he dived low off the banking in his American-built Graham-Page straight eight, during the final lap of an Outer Circuit handicap, to snatch victory from B Burton's impressive 3-litre Talbot by a fifth of a second. In doing so he achieved lasting fame by being the winner of the final motor race to be held there.

A month later war was declared and for the next four years activities at the Surrey track were clothed in secrecy. It was occupied by the Vickers company and used for vital war work. By the time peace came, the famous circuit had been damaged beyond the stage where it could be economically repaired for racing to take place there again.

When this became known there was an immediate outcry that 'it was motor racing, and places like Brooklands, which produced the type of men whose courage had been instrumental in winning the war'. The protests were in vain, however, and after several months of negotiations between the track's owners, Brooklands Weybridge Limited, and the Ministry of Aircraft Production, it was eventually sold.

Before the deal was finalized, Malcolm Campbell, who was a director of the Brooklands company at the time, came in for some heavy criticism from the *Autocar* magazine who wrote: "It is not easy to believe that a man who made his name at Brooklands should now be concerned willingly in negotiations which will deprive this country of the only car-testing ground it has."

The former racing driver and Le Mans hero, Sammy Davis, who was the magazine's Sports Editor, having just returned from the war, was present at the shareholders' meeting when the sale was ratified and Brooklands passed to Vickers for £300,000. As only four per cent of the shares were held by people with motoring and motor racing interests, the result was perhaps a foregone conclusion. Sammy Davis described the meeting as "like sitting in court and hearing an old friend being sentenced to death".

All is not lost, however, and at least some of the spirit of Brooklands lives on following the opening of the Brooklands Museum in 1991 on the 30-acre site, which still contains 24 of the original motoring and aviation buildings. There are plans for a Land Speed Record Exhibition and a Motoring Village, and by the time the Brooklands Centenary takes place in the year 2007 some of the enjoyment and laughter will have returned.

Perhaps then, if visitors close their eyes and use a little imagination, they will be able to hear the crackle of the exhausts and the roar of those magnificent great engines, along with the applause from the crowd, which has been missing since that sunny August day in 1939.

A SQUIRT OF CHAMPAGNE

The attempts by race winners to drench each other in champagne while they are on the rostrum has become a tradition which lovers of good champagne usually watch with a mixture of horror and amazement.

It started by accident at Le Mans in 1966, when Moet et Chandon provided several bottles of their best vintage, to be drunk after the race by the successful drivers and members of the winning team. The bottles were

placed at the back of the winner's rostrum, with the wire removed from their corks, so that they could be opened more easily after the race. It was a very hot day and as the bottles were handed to the drivers a number of the corks flew out. To try to save the contents, some of them put their thumbs across the top, but this only made matters worse and the contents squirted in all directions, soaking everyone in champagne.

The following year, when the drivers were handed the bottles, they again put their thumbs over the top, but gave the contents a good shake to ensure they were able to give each other a good squirt of the stuff. During the past 30 years champagne battles have become a habit after each race, which must delight all the teetotallers watching, but the tradition would surely never have caught on in the days of Le Mans winners like Duncan Hamilton and Ivor Bueb. They knew the true value of champagne and were never known to waste a drop.

CAR THIEVES OLD AND NEW

People were attempting to steal cars as long ago as 1894, when Henry Ford built his first gasoline buggy and had to chain it to a lamp-post whenever he wanted to park, to prevent it from being stolen. It was the first and only car in Detroit at the time, and in 1896, after it had covered about 1,000 miles, he sold it to Charles Ainsley, another Detroit resident, for $200 and repurchased it a year or two later for $100.

At the turn of the century banks in America were only interested in railroads and the public was only interested in speed. In order to gain recognition and get the finance he needed to build more affordable mass-produced cars, Henry Ford had no other choice than to build a car which he could race at the Grosse Point track. With the help of Tom Cooper, he designed and built two single-seaters with large four-cylinder engines producing 80hp and a roar that was said to be quite frightening. He named one The Arrow, for obvious reasons, but his decision to call the other 999 is more obscure.

When Henry Ford drove the 999 at speed he described the experience as being worse than going over Niagara Falls, and he decided to employ Barney Oldfield to drive it in the race he was planning against Alexander

Winton, the American track champion, who had challenged allcomers with his own Winton car.

Although Barney Oldfield was a professional racing cyclist and had never previously driven a car, he had the two qualities Henry Ford was looking for in a driver: he was totally fearless and also had the strength needed to control the two-handed tiller when the car was travelling flat-out. Steering wheels were not in use and racing cars still had tiller steering.

The race took place at Grosse Point and as Barney Oldfield climbed into the seat he waved to the crowd and remarked quite cheerfully: "This challenge may kill me, but at least they will be able to say afterwards that I was going like hell when she took me over the bank."

Henry Ford had made the right choice. Barney Oldfield did drive the 999 flat-out from start to finish, crossing the line nearly half a mile in front of the Winton and advertising the fact that Henry Ford was capable of designing and building a winning car. Seven days later the Ford Motor Company was formed with a capital of $100.

Henry Ford's attempt to stop his first car from being stolen by chaining it to a lamp-post may have been primitive, but it was at least successful. One hundred years later the most sophisticated ultrasonic alarm system fitted to the new £215,000 Bentley Azure failed to prevent car thieves from stealing it one night from an underground garage near Brescia, in Italy.

The breathtaking new 155mph Bentley open-topped tourer, one of the most desirable and expensive cars ever built, had been loaned to Eric Bailey of the *Daily Telegraph* and Alan Copps of *The Times*. They were due to drive it as one of the three support vehicles for the six-strong team of vintage Bentleys taking part in the 1995 *Mille Miglia* road race through 1,000 miles of picturesque Italian towns and villages.

It wasn't the real *Mille Miglia*, which had taken place each year from 1927 until 1957, because that was run on closed roads although it still started and finished at Brescia. The original event came to a sad end when Alfonso de Portago's V12 Ferrari Tipo 335 Sports crashed into the crowd lining the route, killing 10 spectators.

The 1995 *Mille Miglia* also wasn't technically a road race, but a special event for cars built during the 30 years in which the famous race took place. They included magnificent great monsters like the Mercedes SSKs, whose supercharged 7-litre engines produced a wailing scream that would have woken the dead. For the Italians the *Mille Miglia* was a day of worship and many of them were still prepared to line the route for the modern version. Although the Bentleys of the Twenties and Thirties, driven by the legendary

Bentley Boys, never took part in the race, the Rolls-Royce company, having bought the famous marque, decided to give their support to the team of six vintage Bentleys entered by the Benjafield Racing Club.

The club is named after J Dudley Benjafield, a wealthy businessman who won Le Mans in a Bentley in 1920 and then became a member of the Bentley Boys, the group of rich, daring young men who included Sir Henry 'Tim' Birkin, Woolf Barnato and Glen Kidstone. The members of the Benjafield Racing Club carry on their tradition as best they can with their own immaculate pre-1931 Bentleys. For the 1995 *Mille Miglia*, Rolls-Royce supplied them with white overalls, rather like the ones that the Bentley Boys used to wear over their collars and ties when they drove W O Bentley's magnificent machines. The company didn't go so far as to buy the proper fireproof ones, costing about £300 each, but settled for some £14 painters' overalls which they bought from a local supplier at Crewe. Even so, the Bentley drivers certainly looked the part, unlike the members of the official Mercedes team, who had specially tailored overalls which would have done credit to a modern Formula One team.

Anyway, having crossed from England by way of the Channel Tunnel and driven down through France and Switzerland into Italy with their borrowed £215,000 Bentley Azure, Eric Bailey and Alan Copps booked in at a hotel near Brescia, where the event was due to start the following day. They didn't anticipate trouble with car thieves.

Their Bentley, the product of a two-year, £20-million development programme, was fitted with an alarm system capable of detecting even the slightest vibration and would make so much noise in the event of an attempted break-in that it would wake up anyone sleeping in the vicinity, bringing people running to the scene.

The car's automatic transmission system also went into the Park mode, locking the wheels as soon as the engine was switched off, and there was the comforting thought that the Azure weighed more than two tons, was 17ft long, 6ft 2in wide and apart from being one of the most exclusive cars in the world, was unmistakable and very difficult to drive around in unnoticed.

Having ensured that the car was safely locked up for the night, the two motoring editors went off to their hotel, but when they arrived at the garage the following morning, the impossible had happened: thieves had spirited the wonder car away while they slept and the space where it had been left in the hotel's underground car park the previous evening was now occupied by a rather grotty trailer.

Rolls-Royce executives confirmed that the theft was covered by insurance, but that wasn't the most important issue. What really mattered was how the thieves had been able to overcome all the latest technology and smuggle away into thin air one of the world's most exclusive cars without anyone noticing. As it turned out, Henry Ford's ploy 100 years earlier of chaining his car to a lamp-post might have proved as effective, and certainly far cheaper!

Fortunately, the Bentley was found a week or two later after the Italian police had arrested a well-known underworld character who was driving a Mercedes to the Middle East. The thieves must have got cold feet and decided to move the Bentley to a safer hiding place, not far from Linate Airport in Milan. That was where the car was found and it was assumed that the thieves were getting ready to airfreight the stolen Bentley out of the country. The only damage was a slight dent on the rear bumper, probably because the car was so large it might have become wedged against a garage wall.

Apparently, the thieves used some children's modelling putty to put the car's high-tech thief-proof equipment out of action. Modern-day criminals are certainly not short of initiative in their battle of wits with the car makers.

Sir Malcolm Campbell, the World Land Speed record holder and brilliant racing driver, had his own suggestions for dealing with criminals, which unfortunately relied more on flights of fancy than sound engineering practice. He invented a large metal hand with a long telescopic arm to be fitted below the front bumper of a police car. During a chase, as soon as the police car got close enough to the thieves' getaway vehicle, the driver released a lever inside his car and the metal hand with its telescopic arm shot out and grabbed hold of the rear bumper of the car in front.

According to Sir Malcolm, all the police driver had to do then was to brake hard until both vehicles came to a halt. His colleagues should then jump out and arrest the thieves before they could escape.

This was all right in theory, but totally unworkable in practice, so the 'long arm of the law' was another of his inventions which got the thumbs-down.

A BURN-UP WITH A SILVER GHOST

One of the world's most valuable cars nearly went up in smoke during the war when some airmen who were billeted with its owner in Scotland lit a fire in the corner of the motorhouse to keep themselves warm. They certainly did that, but the blaze grew out of control and the flames were leaping round the car, burning the tyres and paintwork before they eventually managed to put the fire out.

The car was a 1907 Rolls-Royce Silver Ghost, built in Manchester for a Mr H R Baird, of Durris House, Kincardineshire, a well-known Scottish landowner. He didn't think that the luxurious, hand-built, saloon body would stand up to the bad roads and rigorous driving conditions in the area, and had it replaced with the eight-seater shooting brake body from his 1906 Coventry-built Maudsley.

This made the car unique and the Silver Ghost's six-cylinder 7,036cc engine gave the shooting brake a top speed of 60mph, at a time when the average saloon could barely reach 20. During the First World War, the back of its polished wooden body was nearly sawn off to make it easier to carry firewood from the hills. It was saved just in time and a double moulding to the rear of the front seat still hides the damage done by a saw.

By 1995 the black, blue and gold Silver Ghost, with its wooden shooting brake body and brass fittings, had a price tag of close on £1,000,000. It is one of only five of the famous models still remaining and its chassis number 577 confirmed that the Auld Lady is the oldest Rolls-Royce still in use.

Apart from being repainted in its original colour scheme, the car is still the same as it was in 1907, except that the previous owner had a 12-volt starter motor and propeller shaft-driven dynamo fitted after he had broken his wrist cranking the engine.

CRASH! BANG! WALLOP!

At a time when cycling was all the rage and the sound of a motor car still brought people rushing to their windows, Billy and Reggie Rootes were fortunate to live in a house where motor cars were the main topic of conversation. Their father was an agent for the Argylls, Clements, Darracqs, de Dions, Humbers, Napiers, Panhards, Stars, Swifts, Vauxhalls and the White Steam Cars, which were famous makes of the day.

William Rootes' workshops at Hawkhurst were full of different models each week, as cars arrived to be sold, serviced, or repaired. Their father also had a successful hire business, providing the local gentry with chauffeur-driven cars for three or four guineas a day, but charging extra for the driver's refreshments. Even more important, as far as his two young sons were concerned, was the gleaming new single-cylinder 1903 New Orleans which William Rootes had bought to take his family on weekend drives into the Kent countryside. Punctures were frequent problems and when there were no more spare wheels left they called at the nearest farm and stuffed the tyres with straw to enable them to reach home. Motoring could be hazardous, it could also be hilarious, but it was certainly never dull.

Despite the hours he spent sitting by the roadside while tyres were changed or repairs took place, those drives in the New Orleans were the highlight of young Billy Rootes' week. By watching his father as they drove along, he soon learned how to work the controls and was keen to have a go himself, but he knew his father would never let a 10-year-old boy drive his prized possession.

Even at that age Billy showed remarkable determination and was quick to take advantage of a situation. The opportunity to drive his father's car came sooner than he expected, when his parents left for London by train one day while the boys were on holiday, leaving the New Orleans in the garage and their two sons in the charge of the maid.

While she was busy upstairs the boys crept into the garage and quietly pushed the car out into the drive. Billy switched on the ignition, and with Reggie working the throttle controls, swung the starting handle as he had seen his father do on many occasions. As soon as the engine roared into life he climbed into the driving seat and, ignoring the shouts of the maid, drove off down the drive.

When they reached the lane he opened up the throttle and the New Orleans began swaying perilously from side to side as they rushed madly down the hill towards the sharp bend at the bottom. Billy seemed oblivious to the danger as his brother pleaded with him to apply the brakes before it was too late. He refused to listen, was fascinated by the car's speed and the sense of power it gave him, but as they approached the bend, he belatedly realized that his brother was right and they were heading for disaster.

The car mounted the grass verge and landed upside-down in the ditch. The boys were thrown clear, but as they picked themselves up and went to investigate the damage, they knew that they were in for a good hiding when their father returned from London.

Fortunately for them, little damage had been done to the New Orleans and Billy had the satisfaction of being able to tell his school friends that he had driven a motor car at speed and had the bruises to prove it. The lesson he learned that day did, however, have an important effect on the close relationship he developed with his brother when they went on to become the most successful partnership in the history of the motor industry.

Billy admitted that although he supplied the motivation for their success, he relied on Reggie to provide the brakes and steering to keep them on the right road. Many of their competitors also claimed that the episode with the New Orleans was the only occasion when Billy didn't listen to Reggie's timely warnings and they fell out together in public.

BUYING SINGERS WITH CHICKENS

When Billy Rootes was 15, he was such a poor scholar that his headmaster persuaded his father to take him away from Cranbrook School and send him to Coventry to join Singer & Company as an apprentice. All the boy seemed interested in was motoring and motor cars and it was certainly a waste of time trying to teach him anything more at school. William Rootes hoped that after his eldest son had completed his five-year apprenticeship, he might have learned enough to be of use in the family motor business in Kent.

While Billy was still at school, William Rootes complained one morning about the price of eggs and agreed to pay for all the food if Billy bought some hens with his savings and provided the family with free eggs each day. He thought the hens would give his wayward elder son something to do and keep him out of mischief. It might also teach him not to enter into rash agreements without first thinking about all the consequences.

What he didn't know was that Billy had thought through the consequences very carefully and was planning to start a chicken farm to supply the village with eggs. He rented a field from a local farmer and, as his father was paying for all the hens' food, he was in a position to sell his eggs cheaper than anyone else and make his chicken farm more profitable. It certainly prospered, so much so that by the end of the school holidays he was able to pay someone to look after the chicken farm for him.

As soon as Billy joined Singer & Company, the school dunce became the star apprentice and, shortly before his eighteenth birthday, he was working in the test shop where the revolutionary new Singer 10 was being put through its paces. It was the country's first real light car which didn't bear any resemblance to a motorcycle, and was destined to become one of the most outstanding models of the decade.

Billy realized that the new car would soon be outselling any rival makes and one morning knocked on the door of the Sales Manager's office and asked if he could have the agency for the Singer 10 in Kent if he placed an order for 50 cars. It was a very unusual request for a young apprentice to make, but the name Rootes meant a great deal in the motor trade, particularly in the Kent area, and young Billy was certainly full of enthusiasm.

Having been told that he could only have the agency if he paid a £5 deposit on each of the 50 cars he had ordered, Billy set off on his motorcycle to see his father at Hawkhurst in the hope of borrowing the £250 from him. As soon as his son told him what he had done, William Rootes flew into a rage and retired to his study where he always kept a number of the musical instruments which had been brought to him for repair. He was a fine musician and whenever he was faced with a difficult situation he found solace in his music.

Billy knew that his father wouldn't change his mind and decided to raise the money by selling his chicken farm for cash to a local farmer, who was impressed by the steady income young Rootes had built up from the sale of eggs in a little over three years.

With the £250 in his pocket, he arrived back in Coventry in time to pay the deposit, order the new Singers and resign his apprenticeship. Within a few weeks he had sold all 50 of the new Singer 10s and made a good profit. He had reached the first rungs on the ladder of success in the motor business and those chickens had started him off.

War came, and while his younger brother Reggie was serving in the Admiralty and looked set for a brilliant civil service career, Billy joined the navy and became Sub-Lieutenant William Rootes, RNVR, attached to the Naval Air Service. When war ended he persuaded his brother to join him. With the help of their father they set up in business together in Kent and formed Rootes Maidstone Limited, with a capital of £1,000, to "carry on the business of aviation, automobile, agricultural and machinery repair experts".

Within two years they were doing so well that they were unable to get enough new cars to satisfy the demand they were creating. The large American motor companies, who had been unfettered by the demands of war, had production to spare and Billy Rootes made his first crossing of the Atlantic to study their business methods and secure the British sales agency for one of the big car companies. The deal he did with General Motors provided the cars they needed and gave them the impetus to develop their business beyond Kent and into other parts of Britain.

It also won them attention from the media. Billy Rootes had seen the value of publicity and the selling power of the press while he was in America, and the brothers organized their own show of imported cars at their Maidstone headquarters. Invitations were sent to all the top motoring writers in London to see and try the latest American models and enjoy some hospitality and entertainment. It was the first time that they had ever been entertained in that way. Chauffeur-driven cars collected them from their Fleet Street offices and took them to Maidstone, where they saw and drove the latest imported models, and after a good lunch they were all taken to the local Point-to-Point races.

Although Billy wasn't much of a horseman, his brother Reggie was and had made a point of studying the ability of all the local horses and riders while he was out hunting each week with the West Kent Foxhounds. He consequently knew those most likely to win and his tips usually paid good odds, so much so that the money won by each of their guests enabled them to be driven back to London after a celebratory dinner with their wallets stuffed with pound notes. Little wonder that invitations from the Rootes brothers were always accepted, and that by the time they had decided to move their headquarters to London in the early Twenties, they already had many friends in the national press.

It was Billy's flair for publicity, as well as his remarkable business acumen, that made the brothers leading figures in the motoring world while they were still young men and enabled them to establish themselves as the largest motor distributors in Britain by the mid-Twenties. Older members of the motor trade didn't like their unusual methods, but the Rootes business flourished at a time when many long-established companies and car makers were going bankrupt.

SOMETHING TO HIDE

Multi-millionaire Lord Rootes was undoubtedly Britain's super salesman, a keen patriot and a successful entrepreneur. He built his remarkable business empire through a mixture of flair, hard work and the ability to generate loyalty from his staff. He never seemed interested in the age of the people he employed, but he always made one stipulation: the men must not have beards. "Never trust anyone with a beard," he told me on several occasions, "it usually means that they are trying to hide something."

On the one occasion he found a member of the Rootes Public Relations staff wearing a beard, he actually was trying to hide something, but not in the way Billy Rootes imagined. Liam Hunter had been working late in Coventry, preparing for a new model launch, but instead of staying overnight as we had planned, he decided to drive back to London in order to keep an early morning appointment. When he fell asleep at the wheel his car went off the road and he was badly cut about the face. He grew a beard to hide the extent of his injuries, until the cuts had healed.

I could guess what Billy Rootes' reaction would be and had tried to keep Liam out of sight as much as possible, but unfortunately he was sitting at his desk one morning when Billy came to see me unexpectedly. Without a moment's hesitation he pointed in the direction of my bearded colleague and said:

"I'd get rid of that man if I were you, John. I don't like the look of him."

"It's Liam Hunter, someone you have always liked," I explained.

"Then why has he got a beard? Tell him to shave it off. It makes him look ridiculous."

With a grunt of annoyance he stomped out before I could explain what had happened.

A few weeks later, after shaving off his beard, Liam came into my office wearing a big grin. Billy Rootes had evidently just met him on the stairs, stared hard at him and said: "Well done Hunter. I'm glad John Bullock persuaded you to get rid of those ridiculous whiskers. A good man like you shouldn't grow a beard. It could ruin a promising career."

"I wonder whether he would remember saying all that about a promising career if I applied for an increase in salary?" Liam asked.

"I wouldn't count on it," I replied.

There were, however, several times when Billy's phobia about beards could have caused serious problems. One occasion was on the eve of an important new model announcement, when the windows at the company's Devonshire House showrooms in Piccadilly were being blacked out to prevent members of the public from seeing the special display of new cars being prepared for the following morning's press reception.

As Billy and I were walking through the showrooms he noticed a tall bearded man standing alongside the main turntable. He was the only one there who still had his coat on and seemed to be taking it easy, while several people in shirt sleeves were busy manoeuvring one of the show cars into position.

"Find out from Elsey who that man is with the beard and tell him to get rid of him. He is the only one with his coat on and not working. We can do without slackers like that."

Bill Elsey was the Rootes Advertising Director who had charge of all the special displays and his harrassed look indicated that all was not going well:

"Who is the man with the beard? Billy wants him fired for slacking," I explained. "You know how he feels about beards."

I thought Bill Elsey was going to explode. "That's all I need!" he exclaimed. "The man he wants to fire is the Managing Director of the company we've employed to provide all the turntables and display material for tomorrow's reception. He's only looked in for a few minutes to check that everything is all right before going out to dinner with his wife. Tell Billy that if I fire him now there won't be any new model display for the press reception tomorrow."

Billy Rootes was waiting for me outside and I gave him the gist of our conversation. He thought for a minute and then shook his head. "I suppose there is nothing we can do then," he said rather gloomily, "but warn Elsey to check through the man's bill very carefully when he gets it."

A DRAG PROBLEM

When Alvis was placed in the hands of the receivers by Cross and Ellis, their coachbuilders, the company made a desperate attempt to get additional finance by building two 12/50 racing cars and entering them for the prestigious 200-mile race at Brooklands in 1923. They were fitted with a new overhead-valve engine designed by George Smith Clarke, the company's Chief Engineer, but the only place they had to test the cars was round the streets of Coventry at night, when everybody had gone to bed.

After a few warming-up laps it was necessary for the harder racing plugs to be fitted by the racing mechanics, who then had to push-start the cars. This took considerable skill and dexterity on the part of the mechanics who had to push using the large rear crossmember which was only about 21 inches from the ground. When the engine fired suddenly and the car shot forward, they were often dragged along until the driver had time to stop. In those days Alvis racing mechanics rarely had any toes to their shoes.

One of the cars driven by Major C M Harvey, known as The Skipper, won the Brooklands 200-Mile Race, lapping at an amazing 95mph and beating the cream of all the foreign teams. The car was taken back to Coventry and loaded onto a horse-drawn dray for a triumphant procession through the

streets before being sent to London to be put on display in the Henlys showrooms.

The Alvis company was saved and went on to build a front-wheel-drive car with the famous red triangle on the bonnet, which caused a sensation when it appeared in 1925, more than 30 years before the front-wheel-drive Mini took the motoring world by storm.

BURMA'S FIRST MOTOR CAR

The large crate in the hold of the *Rawalpindi* caused considerable interest when the ship docked at Rangoon in the summer of 1900, having sailed from England a few months earlier. It was addressed to Rome and Company, the country's main importer of Humber bicycles, but the large crowd who had gathered at the docks to watch the crate being opened knew it contained Burma's first motor car.

It was no secret that a leading Rangoon businessman had read about the Humber Cycle Company's decision to start making motor cars, and had asked his friend George Blackstock, the Chairman of Rome and Company, to order one for him and have it shipped to Burma with the next consignment of bicycles.

The new Humber turned out to be a 3hp, open two-seater Phaeton, but after being removed from its crate, it had to be pushed rather ignominiously along the street to the Rome and Company premises in Fytche Square because although Burma now had its first motor car, there wasn't any petrol!

The car's new owner quite understandably refused to take delivery until he could have a proper test drive and George Blackstock appealed for help from Andrew Campbell, the works manager of the Burma Oil Company, who agreed to try to refine some petrol. After experimenting for several weeks he eventually produced a fluid which smelt and looked something like petrol, but the only lubricating oil available for the Humber was of the type being used for steam engines.

Even then the car's engine wouldn't start, and after everything else had failed, Luck Coon, a Bengali engineer from Calcutta, was sent for to try to get it to work. Swinging the starting handle in accordance with the instructions in the Humber handbook, which had been sent from the factory, had little effect. It was reluctantly decided that the car would have to be shipped back to England, but as it was about to be put back in its crate, Luck Coon suggested that they should have one more try at getting the engine started by putting the car into first gear and pushing it along the street.

The Humber's fuel tank was filled with the remains of Andrew Campbell's petrol concoction, and with the owner at the wheel, everyone got ready to push. Luck Coon sat alongside the driver and was told to "blow the horn like hell if the engine starts". As the vehicle gathered speed, the engine suddenly roared into life and with Luck Coon grinning happily and blowing the horn for all he was worth, they turned into Merchant Street, one of the busiest thoroughfares in Rangoon, particularly on a Saturday afternoon.

As the Humber chugged along at more than 20mph, the driver tried to keep control, doing his best to miss all the Ticca gharries and bullock carts in their path, most of whose drivers were still half asleep after lunch. The teeming mass of pedestrians scattered in all directions as the car zigzagged from one side of the street to another, due partly to its sensitive steering, but also because it was the first time that the driver had been behind the wheel of a moving car.

Merchant Street was soon in an uproar. The Burmese ponies with the gharries and the bullocks pulling the carts bolted with fright at the sight of the Humber coming towards them with its engine racing and Luck Coon sitting in the front, white-faced and still frantically blowing the horn. The driver was too busy trying to steer to work out how to apply the brakes, and it was a miracle that nobody was killed or badly injured as the Humber negotiated Phayre Street and Montgomery Street, before again reaching the

comparative safety of Fytche Square.

After they had completed several circuits of the Square, the engine seized due to overheating and the poor quality of the oil, and the Humber juddered to a halt. The driver turned to congratulate Luck Coon on performing so well on the horn, but before he could do so, his terrified passenger leapt from the car and bolted. It was the last he saw of him. Leaving the Humber where it had come to rest, the shaken driver made for the bar of the Strand Hotel and downed several large brandies before returning home. When he arrived at his office on the Monday morning an official letter from the Rangoon Commissioner of Police was waiting for him, threatening legal action. Their meeting at Police Headquarters later that day was far from harmonious, but the Commissioner agreed to drop all the charges if the owners of the Ticca gharries and bullock carts received generous compensation, particularly for the animals which had been killed or injured during the Humber's erratic passage through the streets of Rangoon. The other stipulation was that Burma's first and only motor car should be shipped back to England as soon as possible.

The first aircraft produced by the Humber company was also exported to Burma in 1909, to fly the mail, after being on show at the Aeronautical Exhibition in London earlier that year. It was touch and go as to whether the aeroplane ever flew at all, after it had been taken to a large field near the Humber factory in Coventry for its inaugural flight. Captain Dawes, one of Britain's most experienced pilots, had agreed to take it up, but on seeing the weird-looking contraption for the first time, retired to the nearest bar and refused to go near the controls until he had been fortified by the contents of a bottle of brandy.

It took several attempts before he managed to get the machine off the ground, and after circling the field once, he landed and climbed from the cockpit still visibly shaken. He refused to go up again despite repeated requests for him to do so by Colonel Cole, the Humber Chairman: "I have got the aircraft down safely and that is all I intend to do" he insisted. Having said his farewells he got into his car and drove away.

Describing the incident some years later, at the Humber company's jubilee celebrations, Colonel Cole admitted: "There is no doubt that it was brandy which got that aircraft into the air, not petrol."

A CAR UNFIT FOR A KING

By 1913 a third of all the new cars sold in Britain were built at Coventry, with Humber, Rover, Swift and Singer being responsible for an incredible 75 per cent of them. Despite the problems the Humber company experienced in Burma, their cars were being sold worldwide, due mainly to the Rootes brothers, who became Humber agents in the Twenties and set up an export business selling only British cars, which stretched from Europe to the Far East.

It was when they couldn't get enough cars to satisfy the demand they had created that the Rootes brothers became motor manufacturers themselves in 1929 and Humber was the first company they bought. Because of their friendship with members of the British royal family and the heads of foreign governments, Humbers were bought by the rich and famous and were used in many parts of the world as the official cars on royal and civic occasions.

Members of the British royal family, Prime Ministers, Government officials, newspaper publishers, company chairmen and famous actors and actresses were Billy Rootes' frequent guests at the weekend house parties and shoots held at Stype Grange, his estate at Hungerford, in Berkshire.

Apart from being an excellent host, he was also a brilliant salesman and it was no coincidence that they nearly all bought Rootes cars.

The Prince of Wales was a frequent visitor to Stype and so was Humphrey Butler, the Duke of Kent's equerry, who was with the Prince of Wales and Mrs Simpson during the trip round the Adriatic which first drew attention to their romance. The Duke of Windsor, when he became King Edward VIII, was responsible for one Rootes model which turned out to be a complete fiasco, and although it appeared at the 1936 Olympia motor show, it was immediately scrapped.

During the years that he had been Prince of Wales the King had been an enthusiastic Humber owner, but he was now being pressurized into using a Daimler as his official car. Rather than let that happen, the Rootes brothers decided to build a ceremonial car which would be bigger and better than any other, but would also appeal to the King's sporting instincts. They gave the challenge to Georges Roesch, who had designed many of the famous Talbots of the Twenties and Thirties, before Rootes bought the company, and he was asked to produce a car, using the largest Humber chassis and a Talbot engine, which would be able to do 100mph. To add some sporting glamour it was decided to call the new model a Sunbeam, a marque famous for its racing successes.

The King was delighted when he heard the news and Billy Rootes kept him informed of the progress of their scheme. Georges Roesch was not happy with the Humber chassis, however, which was already being criticized for its roadholding problems, and the existing six-cylinder Talbot 110 engine had reached its development limits. As far as the engine was concerned, he felt the only answer would be to turn it into a straight-eight, making use of as many of the original components as possible. With the Humber frame stretched to its limits, the larger more powerful engine could just be made to fit and two prototype models were built.

Billy Rootes always insisted on testing every new car himself and had one of the prototypes delivered to him at Stype Grange so that he could take it on holiday with him to Europe. Unfortunately, while he was driving the car near Maidstone, the overstressed chassis broke and he had to wait by the side of the road for a breakdown vehicle to arrive from the company's Maidstone depot. Abandoning the project at that stage would have been even more embarrassing, but King Edward VIII's abdication saved the situation for Rootes. Although the model did appear at the London motor show, the prototypes were scrapped, along with the company's plans to put the model into production!

UPSTAIRS DOWNSTAIRS

A Swiss designer invented a car in 1904 which he claimed could pass through the doors of a normal house and be taken upstairs by people living in flats, instead of having to be parked outside in the street.

Martin Fischer's Turicum car was only 70 inches long and had the engine situated ahead of the front wheels, which the driver steered with his feet. The rear-mounted fuel tank also acted as a backrest for the single seat which was mounted on the chassis in front of the rear wheels.

A lever either side of the seat controlled the brake and gear change, leaving the driver's hands free to blow the horn and fend off pedestrians if they got in his way.

Little wonder that the Swiss motor industry never really took off and the country's inventive genius was soon being channelled in other directions.

ACHTUNG!
BASTARD SPITFIRE

Billy Rootes was sent to Coventry by Winston Churchill on the morning of November 15, 1940, after German bombers had torn the heart out of the place and almost demolished several of the car factories which were essential to the war effort. His task was to bring new life into the badly shocked city and get production going again as quickly as possible.

He stood on an upturned box outside the factory gates, encouraging the workforce to clear up the mess, and promised that they would soon have their own means of hitting back at the German Air Force which had wrought such havoc to Coventry.

When he returned to London he paid for three Spitfires and became President of an appeal to raise the £100,000 needed for the motor industry to have its own fighter squadron. Viscount Nuffield, Lord Austin, Lord Perry and Lord Kenilworth all became patrons and H G Starley, of Champion

Sparking Plugs, agreed to become Secretary.

Large sectional drawings of a Spitfire were used in factories and schools so that people of all ages could become involved. A rivet cost sixpence, a sparking plug eight shillings, a petrol tank £40, an engine £2,000 and a complete aircraft £5,000. Before long, enough money had been raised to buy 21 Spitfires and the Motor Industry Squadron went into action. Many of the aircraft were named after motor companies and individual makes of car, and because of the squadrons' coat of arms, with the bar sinister, its pilots became known as the 'bastards of the air'.

Until the squadron was disbanded in April 1945 it was in the thick of the fighting in the skies over Britain and also did two years' service overseas.

A GUN-HAPPY DETECTIVE AND WINSTON'S PIGS

Whenever Harold Macmillan went shooting at Sir William Rootes' estate at Hungerford there was always tight security and scrambler telephones had to be installed, just in case any urgent affairs of state had to be dealt with while the Prime Minister was potting away at Billy's pheasants. I was in Coventry, photographing some of the company's new cars with Ronnie Clayton and his colleagues, when a message arrived that the Chairman had a number of very important guests due and would like some photographs taken during that day's shoot. I had been tipped off that Harold Macmillan would be among the guests and suggested to Ronnie that on this occasion he should go and take the photographs himself.

There wasn't time for him to go home to change into something more suitable, but Ronnie knew his way around and when he arrived there he managed to persuade the valet to loan him some of Sir William's own clothes. The valet also offered him the choice of several pairs of shooting boots, which were neatly arranged in rows along one of the walls of the gun room. By the time he had been kitted out by the valet, Ronnie Clayton was one of the best dressed people at the shoot. On several occasions during the morning Sir William looked rather intently at him and after lunch came up and said:

"I've been admiring those boots you are wearing, Clayton. They are very

like a pair I have and you must make sure you look after them."

Later that afternoon the guns were standing at the bottom of a valley, near to some woods on the edge of the estate, when several pistol shots rang out. Several of the guests thought an attempt had been made on the Prime Minister's life and pandemonium broke out, until he appeared unscathed with his personal detective holding a revolver and looking rather sheepish. The detective admitted that he had become rather bored watching everybody else doing the shooting and decided to use his revolver to take some pot shots at some hares which had popped up out of the undergrowth. The hares escaped, but the pistol shots went very close to some beaters who were working their way along the other side of the bank. The detective was full of apologies and promised to put his revolver away for the remainder of the afternoon, leaving the Prime Minister and the other guests to do the shooting.

There was also a close friendship between Sir William Rootes and Winston Churchill, and during the time that he was Prime Minister, their common interest in farming and cars led to an unfortunate lapse of security over one new Rootes model several months before it was due to be announced, causing considerable consternation among the sales staff and Rootes dealers. The new model was the first Humber estate car and many newspapers carried pictures of the prototype when Churchill was photographed with it on several occasions during his painting holiday in Italy. Fortunately, it was all Sir William's own fault and he had nobody else to blame.

Sir William's insistence on trying every new model himself before it went into production went back to the time of the first Hillman Minx in 1930. He liked to make sure that the designers had done their job properly, and as he was planning to spend the following weekend at his estate near Hungerford, he arranged for the prototype of the new estate car to be delivered to him there, where it would be well away from any prying eyes. Stype was quite a large estate, with several large farms, a nine-hole golf course, an indoor swimming pool and squash court and some excellent shooting. The house itself was not particularly large, because the original Stype Grange had been burned to the ground under rather mysterious circumstances in 1930, when it was owned by Lord Marchamley's son, the Hon Ronald Whiteley.

Ronnie Whiteley and his wife had left their butler in charge while they went for a long holiday in South Africa, but when their ship docked at Southampton several months later, the butler met them with the news that Stype Grange had burned to the ground the previous night. He explained that he, his wife and child had narrowly escaped death, fighting the fire until the arrival of the fire brigade, but despite all their efforts, none of the contents of the house had been saved. The Whiteleys were understandably very upset, but accepted their butler's story and decided to move into one of the cottages until a new house could be built.

It was only when some friends of theirs recognized a piece of furniture in an antique shop as having come from Stype Grange that the police were asked to investigate. They found several other antiques belonging to the Whiteleys and traced them all back to the butler, who admitted selling them. The police were sure that the fire was intended to hide the thefts, but never had sufficient proof. The butler was found guilty of theft, however, and spent several years in prison. The Whiteleys were so distressed over the affair that they decided to move and sold the estate to Billy Rootes. He later sold it to Sir Charles Clore and bought Ramsbury, a larger estate nearby with a magnificent house and lake.

During the weekend that Billy Rootes was testing the prototype of the new estate car at Stype, he had a call from Winston Churchill inviting him to Chequers on the Sunday, to see some pigs which he was anxious to buy. Although the drive to Chequers would provide a good opportunity to test the new estate car more thoroughly, Billy was worried about it being seen, but he had no other choice because it was the only car available as the chauffeur had taken his Humber Pullman to be serviced.

When he arrived at Chequers he parked the prototype out of sight of the house and rang the bell. He was met by Winston's son Randolph who, according to Billy, explained, "You'll find father in the library writing one of his impromptu speeches."

After lunch Churchill took Billy to see the pigs and then insisted on walking with him back to his car.

"What's that you've got?" Churchill wanted to know. "You must take me for a ride in it, Billy. It's just what I need for my painting holiday."

Billy Rootes tried to explain that it was the prototype of a new model which would not be available for several months, but Churchill wouldn't listen.

"Rubbish, Billy" he insisted. "This is just perfect as it is. I start my painting holiday in Italy next week and if I can't have your Humber, you can't have my pigs and the deal's off."

Billy knew there was little point in arguing. Churchill had made up his mind and he was used to getting his own way. The prototype estate car was delivered to Chequers the following day and despatched to Italy with all his paints and canvases. During the next few weeks there were almost daily reports of him perched alongside it, painting happily away, seemingly oblivious of the interest he was creating in the car.

Billy tried to pass off loaning Churchill the prototype Humber as a brilliant piece of public relations on his part. He had certainly ensured that the company's new estate car achieved more worldwide media coverage than it would otherwise have done, and I suppose I should have been grateful that he didn't expect the public relations department to pay for the pigs!

Churchill continued to buy Humbers until Rootes stopped making their luxurious, top-of-the-range Pullman models and tore out the assembly line at Coventry where they had been built, in order to make space for a new mass-production model. When this happened, Churchill was forced to change his old Humber Pullman for a new Rolls-Royce, undoubtedly a very fine car in many ways, but it didn't have anything like as much room in the back. Churchill wasn't able to stretch out his legs and relax during the long journeys as he had been able to do in his old car.

He telephoned Billy Rootes to say that he had to have another Pullman and didn't want to be told that he couldn't. The fact that the assembly line had been dismantled and production of the model had ceased several months earlier made no difference.

"I'm sure you could build one for me if you tried," he insisted. "Don't forget that I'm one of your best customers and have been for a long time. You can't let me down now, I need another Pullman that I can stretch out in."

Billy agreed to see what could be done, but as all the jigs and tools had been destroyed, a new car was out of the question. He gave orders that the company should buy a low-mileage Pullman and send it to the Humber factory to be completely stripped down and rebuilt, piece by piece, until it was as good as new. By the time it was finished it must have been the most costly Humber ever built, but Churchill got his car and Billy Rootes kept his promise. Churchill was delighted and never sold his last hand-made Pullman. He still owned it when he died many years later.

THE OVERALL PROBLEM

One of the most colourful characters in the motor industry after the war was Alan Hess, the Publicity Manager for the Austin Motor Company. He was short and stocky, with a liking for the good life, and was a familiar sight at motoring events in his white convertible, usually smoking a fat cigar and accompanied by two very attractive models in case a photographer wanted to take a picture of the car. He rarely missed a trick when it came to getting publicity for the Austin Motor Company, and found a novel way of getting round the BBC's insistence that company names mustn't be mentioned, even when they were filming in a factory.

He had arranged for the BBC to film the new Austin models coming down the assembly lines at Longbridge for a programme on the motor industry that was going out live that evening.

Everything went smoothly during rehearsals, with all the assembly line workers dressed in their usual dirty overalls. The producer had also carefully situated his cameras so that they would miss all the Austin Motor Company notices which Alan had arranged to be placed at strategic points in the factory, but the PR man wasn't to be thwarted and still had another trick up his sleeve.

Just as the programme went on the air he gave the signal and all the assembly workers changed from the dirty overalls they had been wearing into new white ones with the Austin name and logo clearly visible. There was nothing the BBC could do and they had to carry on with the programme, but Alan Hess had ensured that nobody watching was left in any doubt that they were at the Austin Motor Company's factory and it was their new cars which were being filmed.

Alan Hess had clearly had the last laugh, even though the BBC complained to the Austin management about sharp practice on the part of the company's Publicity Manager. They also refused to do any more live programmes at the factory while Hess was still in charge.

A WOMAN'S INFLUENCE

Motor manufacturers who don't have women in their design teams would now be accused of sexual descrimination, political incorrectness and no doubt several other modern-day preoccupations, but in the days when motoring was a male preserve and women were expected to take a back seat, it was all very different. Not until the Austin Motor Company invited the delectable Kay Petre to become their colour consultant in 1954 did a single manufacturer attempt to put any serious female input into car design. Kay was asked to choose materials and colours for the new Austin Cambridge and was then featured in the company's newspaper and magazine advertising, but most other manufacturers looked upon the move as just another sales gimmick, which the company eventually dropped.

Apart from being frequently referred to as the 'First Lady of Motor Racing', Kay clocked up several other important firsts and was a household name for more than 40 years. She was certainly one of the most glamorous drivers to thrill the crowds at the famous Brooklands race track in the Thirties, and as a boy I spent many weekends there with my father, watching her and other great drivers like Sir Malcolm Campbell winning races, setting new records and riding high on the famous banking.

Kay's racing career began soon after she married Henry Petre, a well-known Brooklands pilot, and won a ladies' race in the Wolseley Hornet he gave her as a birthday present. She knew how to get what she wanted and soon persuaded him to buy her a 2-litre Bugatti so that she could compete on equal terms with the men, and then broke the Brooklands outer circuit ladies' lap record in it at 124.14mph. The following Saturday, at the wheel of a monster 10½-litre Delage, she raised the record to 129.58mph. Kay was so petite that before she could drive the car it had to be fitted with a special seat and longer pedals.

Her record didn't last long, however, because on the Bank Holiday Monday Gwenda Stewart went round the circuit at 135.95mph in her 1½-litre, supercharged straight-eight Derby front-wheel-drive single-seater racer. The fact that Mrs Stewart's remarkable record was never beaten is a tribute to the spirit and skill of the women racers of the day.

Lord Austin was so impressed with Kay's courage and ability that he invited her to drive a works single-seater Austin Seven, along with Bert Hadley and Charles Goodacre, making her the first woman to join a factory team. Seventeen drivers were awarded the coveted badge for lapping Brooklands at more than 130mph and Kay Petre and Gwenda Stewart were the only women to do so.

Kay's remarkable motor racing career sadly came to an end in September 1937 during practice for the BRDC 500-mile race, when a single-seater MG Magnette, driven by Reg Parnell, hit the retaining wall and slid down the Brooklands banking, crashing into Kay's works Austin Seven, rolling it over and throwing her out onto the track.

As soon as she had recovered from the serious injuries caused by the accident, Kay joined the *Daily Sketch* and became the first woman motoring correspondent of a national daily newspaper. Although no longer racing, she narrowly escaped death again in 1939 when she was reporting the Monte Carlo Rally for her paper with her colleague Major Reggie Empson. He was killed in France when their car and a lorry collided at a crossroads on their way to Digne. Kay received serious facial and other injuries during what was to be the last Monte Carlo Rally for 10 years. The accident left her badly scarred and with a paralyzed muscle in her face, but even so she was still very good-looking and kept the lovely figure which helped to make her the darling of the crowds during her racing career.

The famous Austin Seven Grasshopper racing car, which Kay was the first to drive in competitions, was returned to the road in 1995 after an interval of some 45 years. Her historic car, COA 119, was one of about 12 of the small, supercharged, Austin Seven racers made around 1937 and was finished in blue, Kay's favourite colour. It is owned by John Wilson, a Dunoon garage owner, whose parents bought him the car in 1939, and after the war he drove it successfully in hillclimbs and other events.

After 1950 it fell into disrepair and lay in the corner of his garage for some years. It was eventually sent to the Austin factory for repair, but the work was never finished. During the Leyland era it was returned to Dunoon in a parts van and eventually dismantled. Fortunately for vintage car enthusiasts, John Wilson decided to have it restored in time for the 1995 Cream Cracker Rally and it is once again in pristine condition.

After the war, Kay Petre's election as the first woman member of the Guild of Motoring Writers led to some embarrassing incidents when car manufacturers and some of her own colleagues forgot that she had become a fully-fledged member of what they had always considered to be a man's world. It was certainly brought home to her colleagues in July 1951, when Leonard Lord, the Austin Motor Company Chairman, invited some of the leading British motoring writers to test-drive his company's new Austin A40 during a fact-finding trip across Canada. He was particularly angry at the way in which many of the papers, mine included, had been critical of the performance of British cars in overseas markets.

Everything was going according to plan until Kay's male colleagues came across the tempting waters of a lake after a long, sticky drive across the Rockies. When they reached a quiet spot in one of the forest clearings, they parked their cars, stripped off their clothes and dived naked into the cooling water. Kay, who was sharing the driving with Dudley Noble of *Milestones* magazine and Ken Obank of the *Sunday Observer*, was some way behind because she had insisted upon stopping to tidy up the inside of their car and get rid of all the rubbish, including the old wine bottles and over-ripe remains of the fruit they had collected during the trip.

As a result the bathing party was in full swing by the time they arrived on the scene and several of the motoring writers were running around in the nude, trying to dry off after their swim. When they realized that Kay was

watching their antics with some considerable amusement, they either made a bee-line for their cars, or dived into the lake and remained there until she had driven on. Kay was probably the only woman motoring correspondent who could claim to have seen many of her male colleagues in the nude, but which of them she saw naked in Canada that day she kept secret until her death in August 1994 at the age of 91.

There were other occasions when Kay's presence at an otherwise all-male gathering gave rise to some amusing situations, particularly when comedians, brought in by motor manufacturers to entertain the press at new model launches, had to change their act at the last moment when they came on stage and saw a lone woman sitting in the audience. In fairness to Kay, she would have preferred it if they had gone ahead with their usual routine and not treated her any differently from her male colleagues. It was usually the motor company executives who were the more embarrassed.

Apart from the brief period when she was involved with the styling team at Austin, new models continued to be designed by men who had little or no real knowledge of what women wanted or needed. This was evident when Rootes produced the Mark III Sunbeam, which went on to become an outstanding rally car in the hands of many women drivers, including Sheila Van Damm.

At the launch party in London I invited Carole Carr, the well known singer and television personality, who was a keen Rootes owner, to try our new model. When she insisted that even with the driving seat as far back as possible there still wasn't enough room behind the wheel for her legs, I thought she was joking, but she was right: our all-male design team had overlooked the fact that while men always drive with their legs apart, most women drive with their knees together! Although our test drivers, some of whom were over six feet and weighed more than 16 stones, found plenty of room for their legs and bulky frames, if one of the testers been a woman, the necessary changes to the driving position would have been made before the car went into production and a lot of money would have been saved. As soon as we realized the problem, the rake of the steering column was altered and modifications were carried out on the cars already in dealers' hands.

•

GIMMICK TIME FOR NEW MODELS

Thanks to Carole Carr, what would certainly have been a more embarrassing and costlier situation was prevented when the new Mark III Sunbeam went into full production. The model went on to become a top rally car and a popular choice with women drivers, as well as with the men. Apart from being a successful singer, Carole starred in several popular television shows and helped us with the launch of a number of other new models, but a gimmick we planned during a photographic session at the RAC Country Club at Woodcote Park, near Epsom, for the launch of the Singer Gazelle nearly ended in tragedy and the sort of publicity we didn't want.

The manager of Painton Zoo had offered me the use of a lamb and lion cub who had been born and brought up there together. I was assured that the lion cub was very tame and wouldn't present any problem and that the lamb was well able to look after itself when they played together. The idea of photographing them both with our new Gazelle and another famous singer did seem to have possibilities and I eventually agreed to the zoo's proposal.

Maybe I had taken too long in making a decision, but when the animals arrived and were removed from their travelling cages, the lion club and lamb were both rather bigger than I had expected. Even so the keeper who had brought them from Painton that morning again assured me that we had nothing to worry about.

To begin with he seemed to be right and Carole, who had understandably been rather hesitant at first, entered into the spirit of the occasion, playing with both animals and having close-up shots taken with the lion cub on the bonnet of the Gazelle.

The accident which I had feared might happen occurred when we called a halt for lunch and the keeper took the lamb and lion cub back to their cages to be fed. He came staggering back a few minutes later, looking very pale and with blood streaming from several deep gashes in both of his arms. We used towels to try to stop the bleeding and rushed him off to hospital. Fortunately, despite all the mess, he was not badly injured and was allowed home after treatment, but the situation would have been much more serious if the lion cub had turned on Carole while they had been playing together only a few minutes earlier. I never used wild animals again and stuck to two-legged models for all our new car photography.

A MODEL LAUNCH

The car should, of course, always be the star at every new model announcement, but there was one launch when I decided to do away with the car altogether. It was when our plans to announce a new Hillman Minx had been ruined at the last minute by the severe petrol rationing brought about by the Suez crisis, and all thoughts of the usual press launch and road tests had to be abandoned until petrol rationing was lifted. Having worked hard on all the preliminaries, my colleagues and I had been looking forward to spending a week or two in the sun attending the press launch planned for the South of France. The abandonment came as a big anti-climax for us and many of our friends in the motoring press.

I was having a drink one evening with Ronnie Clayton, who had just finished photographing the new car, when an idea emerged for a different kind of new model launch which wouldn't be affected by petrol rationing. We were in the downstairs bar of London's Ritz hotel, known affectionately as the 'pink sink', a favourite watering hole for Rootes' executives. The bar was also popular with a number of wealthy visitors from overseas, several of whom knew that Laurie, the head barman, was surprisingly an authority on paintings and a regular visitor to the sale rooms at Christie's and Sotherby's on his days off. He was frequently commissioned by them to buy important paintings and his wife was also a talented picture restorer. Their London flat was filled with the fine pictures which Laurie had bought for himself and those due for restoration.

When Ronnie Clayton and I arrived at the Ritz that evening, instead of being a hive of activity as it usually was at that time, the downstairs bar was almost empty. It was Friday night and due to the petrol shortage most people had left early to catch trains, having had to leave their cars at home. A couple of Laurie's special cocktails had a cheering effect on us and we began to look on the bright side. Even if the Government had put paid to the official announcement of the company's new model, at least for the time being, we decided that we should do something to lift the spirits of our colleagues and motoring friends by launching a special new model of our own, which would feature many of the car's outstanding assets.

The following Monday we visited several leading model agencies and eventually found the one we were looking for. She was also a new model, tall and shapely – with a body which couldn't be matched by even the most talented car designer. When we met her later that week it was clear that she was just about perfect for the part and seemed very keen to enter into the spirit of the model launch we had in mind.

The photographs we needed for our own new model brochure were taken in Ronnie Clayton's studio and every pose was done "in the best possible taste" as Kenny Everett would have said. Each one illustrated the main features of the model we were unable to launch: its clean lines, a stylish front and an attractive rear end as well as independent front suspension, the ability to park neatly and a high quality finish.

We replaced the photographs of the cars in the official Minx brochure with those of our own new model, but kept the same descriptive copy. When everything was ready we held our own launch party and gave everybody one of our special new model brochures.

We were certainly surprised by the response to what we had intended as a joke. News of the brochure spread like wildfire. It was before the famous Pirelli calendars, and the calls to the Rootes Public Relations Department asking for copies started the following day. Some came from motoring writers who had been at the party, asking if they could have a copy for their news editors; others came from Rootes' dealers who had heard about the brochure and wanted copies to help cheer-up some of their more important customers who were also fed up with petrol rationing. We also had calls from several Rootes car owners, who had heard on the grapevine about the special 'Miss Minx' brochure and wanted to know if their local dealers would be having copies. There were even calls from MPs and members of the House of Lords, claiming to be personal friends of the Rootes family and long-time Rootes owners.

We printed several hundred extra copies, but the demand grew and we had to impose our own rationing system. My secretary became very adept at sorting out the genuine callers from those who were trying to acquire copies under some false pretext. One main dealer offered to pay the printing bill if I would let him have some additional copies for a fleet customer who had promised an order for 50 vehicles in return. He got his copies and the dealer got the order. I don't know how many other sales our special brochure was responsible for during that difficult period, but it certainly created a considerable amount of amusement and goodwill – except among those who couldn't get a copy.

My colleagues and I were also glad that our delightful model benefited from the brochure. She was in great demand as a result of all the interest and went on to have a successful modelling career.

CLOCKING OFF

Presenting people with a gold watch or a clock when they retired was at one time the custom in the motor industry, as if they didn't have enough time on their hands. Bill Batty's retirement as Chairman of the Ford Motor Company was marked by many gestures of goodwill from friends and colleagues.

Among the parcels which arrived through the post at his office at Warley one morning was a largish brown package addressed to Sir William Batty and marked 'Personal'. When his secretary placed it on his desk she was sure she could hear a rather ominous ticking. At the time the IRA had been threatening to target well-known people in Britain and it looked as though the package might well contain a bomb as a going-away present.

The ticking parcel was rushed outside and the police were called. They immediately alerted the Army's bomb squad, who arrived a few minutes later, took one look at the mysterious object and decided not to take any unnecessary risks. There was then a muffled explosion – and a rather fine carriage clock ticked for the very last time. An embarrassed young army officer was left to gather up the bits.

The clock had been a farewell present from a grateful Ford dealer association, but someone had unfortunately given it a wind to make sure that it worked properly, before posting it. There must have been enough tension left in the spring to set the mechanism ticking again after the clock had been delivered.

Still, a valuable carriage clock was perhaps not the wisest present to send through the post to a leading British industrialist at such a sensitive time.

A TRIPLE EIGHTY

There was little thought of taking things easy for Major Tom May, a former racing driver and Army pilot, when he decided to celebrate his 80th birthday in 1995 by driving his 1952 Aston Martin DB2 at more than 80mph for 80 minutes, in support of the Aston Martin Owners Club's Diamond Jubilee celebrations.

Accompanied by his racing mechanic, Charlie Sheppard, an Aston Martin and Lagonda restoration expert, he completed 55 laps of the oval, two-mile high-speed banking at Millbrook Proving Ground in Bedfordshire.

The Aston Martin Owners Club was formed in May 1935 when a small group of enthusiasts met at the Grafton Hotel, Tottenham Court Road, in London. Major May also got his first Aston Martin in 1935, when his parents gave him a 1930 International model for his 19th birthday.

After three motorcycle accidents he persuaded his parents that he would be safer on four wheels, but when they wanted to buy him the vicar's Austin Seven, he agreed to put £15 of his own money towards the £60 the owner wanted for the Aston Martin!

THEY SOUGHT THE DAUPHINE EVERYWHERE

The attractive little Renault Dauphine had one of the best car launches of the Fifties and the catchy little jingle used to publicize the name was hummed and whistled across Europe by people of all ages. The existence of the car was kept a closely guarded secret, but several months before it was due to be announced, panic broke out in the Renault camp when photographs appeared in *L'Auto Journal*, the French motoring magazine famous for its new model 'scoops'.

An immediate inquiry was held as to how such tight security could have been breached, particularly as nearly all the testing of the new model had been restricted to the company's own heavily guarded engineering facilities near Paris. Apart from the high wire fence surrounding the proving ground, the area was patrolled night and day by guard dogs and there hadn't been any reports of break-ins, or even any suspicious circumstances.

The Renault design team and development engineers, although questioned, were beyond suspicion and the loophole in security remained a mystery for more than 20 years until it was revealed that a determined photographer had resorted to the same method which hundreds of POWs had used successfully during the war to escape from German prison camps.

He and his accomplices had succeeded in digging a tunnel under the perimeter fence. The entrance was hidden by some bushes, but was just big enough for him to wriggle through with his camera and take shots of the prototype Dauphine models undergoing tests. He'd even managed to achieve some close-ups of the cars while they were left unguarded inside the proving ground and nobody thought there was any danger to security. The photographer and his assistants must have got the idea from watching all those war films, but his tunnel was never discovered, probably because he was breaking in, not out.

When the company took the prototypes to Portugal for some more secret testing, to keep the Dauphine away from any other prying photographers the cars were taken by truck and unloaded at night at the little railway station of *St Jean Pied De Port*, near the Spanish border.

A week later, when they were being reloaded, again during the night and at the same railway station, several *gendarmes* arrived and wanted to know what was going on. Having been caught in the act, there was little point in not telling them the truth, but the reaction of the *gendarmes* came as a surprise. They just laughed and said: "We thought that is what you might be doing. Your friends at Citroen have been doing the same thing here with their new model!"

Another prototype was taken to St Nazare for a film company to make a promotional film of the car. They hired a helicopter so that the Dauphine could be filmed at various different angles while it was being driven along the coast and harbour by a pretty girl. The pilot was able to fly around the car while the camera crew filmed it from all angles. What he didn't know,

however, was that the model driving the Dauphine had never been taught to drive and didn't even have a driving licence! She had obviously hidden the fact from the film company in order to get the job.

Had the pilot known, he wouldn't have been hovering close to the car, a few feet from the ground, for some frontal shots to be taken. He was taken by surprise when the girl's foot slipped off the brake pedal onto the accelerator and the car suddenly shot forward, smashing into the helicopter and bringing it crashing to the ground. Fortunately nobody was seriously hurt, but both the prototype and the helicopter were complete write-offs.

When the insurance company was asked to pay up they refused to do so because their policy stipulated that the Dauphine should only be driven by someone with a full licence. As the girl didn't have a driving licence at all, the film company was faced with a bill for damages running into more than £250,000, which took them several years to settle. Not many motorists can claim to have brought down a helicopter.

Corsica was chosen for the press launch of the car and every few days small groups of French and foreign motoring journalist were flown there, to road-test the Dauphine and enjoy the gastronomic delights of the establishment owned by Charlot Pardi, a restaurateur with a fine cellar of wines and a wonderfully dry sense of humour. When asked by one foreign journalist in a rather derogatory manner whether it was true that he had never left Corsica, he replied poker-faced:

"That is certainly not true. I leave the island every week. I am a fisherman."

The small armada of cars and company personnel which arrived at Ajaccio in December included the six Renault Dauphines which had been despatched from the factory in crates, with the intention of ensuring strict secrecy. Instead they attracted considerable curiosity all the way along the route from the factory, particularly at Marseilles, where the port officials insisted on a thorough inspection of every crate.

The four works drivers arrived separately, along with six mechanics, a photographer, the PR chief Bob Sicot and his assistant Roger Steigelmann, and Louis Fromentin, one of company's test engineers, who had been a member of the team which broke the world 24-hour record with a Renault 4CV at the Montlhery track.

The test cars were all stored in a large warehouse, which was meant to be empty when they arrived, but still contained a large stock of rice that had been left there by a previous occupant. As a result, the mechanics working on the cars had to contend with an army of well-fed rats which came to watch the proceedings each day with obvious interest. The rats proved to be quite friendly, however, and in the end it was decided to leave them in peace.

Even so, the cars were all locked up each night and carefully checked over before they left the warehouse in the morning, to make sure that none of the rats accompanied the journalists on their test-drives. If one had suddenly appeared in the passenger seat, the result could have been quite spectacular.

For nearly two months, parties of journalists arrived at *Campo dell'Oro*, which could hardly be described as an airport. The terminal buildings consisted of two wooden barns situated in a field where Bob Sicot and his parents had picked mushrooms during the war. Each group of journalists was taken to the south of the Gulf of Ajaccio as soon as they landed, to see the picturesque display of Renault Dauphines, which had been arranged in a small clearing in the *maquis*, a Corsican thicket now the site of a luxurious Sofitel hotel.

There weren't any large hotels on the island then and everyone stayed at a small hotel by the sea. The following morning the journalists were able to drive the cars across the mountains with a choice of three different routes. The roads were extremely narrow and winding, however, making the testing so nerve-wracking that the plan to put a company engineer in each car was quickly dropped. Being a passenger while the cars were being put through their paces by some of the journalists was looked upon by the engineers as being altogether too dicey.

At the end of each day there was a party. A Swiss journalist became very amorous one evening at the Cafe Napoleon after drinking too much Corsican wine, and a number of local women complained that he wouldn't keep his hands to himself and made suggestive remarks which they found offensive.

His surname in German meant 'lover of ladies', which proved to be rather apt as the evening wore on. When the situation looked as though it was really getting out of hand, the Public Relations man in charge of the Swiss party assured Bob Sicot that he knew what to do, and would get the journalist safely off to bed within the next 10 minutes or so. He proved quite right and not long afterwards led the 'lover of ladies' with the wandering hands quietly to his room. The man wasn't seen again until the following afternoon.

"What did you say to him?", Bob asked the Swiss PR man, when he returned to the party a few minutes later.

"I didn't have to say anything," was the surprising reply. "I know him well and when he really begins to misbehave himself and looks like causing serious trouble, I just slip a couple of sleeping tablets into his wine. When they start to work I take him to his room to sleep and he doesn't give anybody any further trouble. I usually apologize on his behalf to the women he has offended, offer them a drink, which they usually accept, and everybody is happy again. It's all part of the job."

A radio station covering the launch wanted to include someone with a very pronounced Corsican accent to give some local colour to their report. With Charlot Pardi's help, Bob Sicot found a local man who played his part well and quite enjoyed his moment of radio glory. A year or two later, during another visit to the island, Bob inquired what had happened to the man.

"Oh sadly he's no longer with us", came the reply. "He got involved with the Mafia and some cigarette smuggling and was slightly shot!"

More than 300 journalists visited Corsica as guests of Renault, and the Dauphine launch gave birth to the *Tour de Corse* Rally. The decision was made after several bottles of *Patrimonio*, a local Corsican wine, had been drunk by a group of rally enthusiasts during dinner one evening.

Many motoring journalists on overseas press visits owed a debt of gratitude to Boris Zvetkoff, one of the finest barmen in Europe, who looked after everyone at Renault press parties for nearly 25 years. He knew them all, their likes and dislikes and how to cure their hangovers the following morning when they had drunk too much of the local wine. He had been the barman at the American Legion in Paris and got the Renault job when he replied to an advertisement placed in a wine trade journal by Bob Sicot's cousin, who owned a hotel at *Saint Laurent* which was being used for the launch of the Renault Floride. Renault wanted an experienced barman to look after the foreign press, who had charm, a sense of humour and spoke several languages. Boris had all those qualifications.

He was born in Moscow and his distinguished looks added strength to the rumour that he came from a Russian family of noble birth. All Boris would say was, "I may be the son of a Grand Prince, or I may be the son of a road sweeper. I prefer not to know." A party of German motoring journalists spread the news of his possible noble birth after Boris and Bob had enlivened a dull evening by insisting on toasting all the Romanoffs, the Russian imperial family, in vodka. The Germans joined in and the names Boris didn't know he made up, until they had run out of vodka.

When he eventually stopped working for Renault he became barman at a popular restaurant situated in the basement of the FFSA, the French Automobile Sports Association, in Paris. He is now buried in the Russian Cemetary at Nice, alongside a member of the Russian imperial family. It is to be hoped that Boris approves of his final resting place.

There are many more motoring journalists and motoring magazines now than there were at the end of the war, when new model road-testing really began. The larger motor manufacturers seem to be looking farther and farther afield each year in their search for more exotic places in which to film their cars and hold their new model extravaganzas. As a result, motoring journalists sometimes have to spend almost as much time in the air as they do behind the wheel of a new car, and new model launches have lost much of their intimacy. They are now usually more serious affairs and have sadly become much less fun.

PLENTY OF SPACE BUT NO SHUTTLE

There was certainly no lack of imagination on the part of the Fiat company when they launched their new Uno, which must have been the biggest launch programme ever undertaken by a motor manufacturer. They chose Florida, and two specially chartered Boeing 747s airlifted more than 1,000 journalists across the Atlantic, while scores of Unos were shipped to America for the press to drive.

During a week which included road-tests, demonstrations and an opportunity to drive the Uno on the famous banking of the Daytona Speedway, there were the impressive engineering presentations at the Kennedy Space Centre and a major teleconference, with satellite links to various European capitals enabling journalists to speak to Vittorio Ghidella, Fiat's head of car operations in Turin. Motoring writers, however, have always stressed the value they place on a close personal contact with company chiefs, and many of them were not over-impressed by the technicalities of the launch.

The opportunities they had to savour some of the tourist delights of Florida were also spoilt to some extent because it rained all the time, and no amount of modern technical wizardry could solve that age-old problem. The climax of the week was intended to be the launch of the space shuttle, but the poor weather conditions caused a change of plan and a last-minute postponement.

Even so, the Uno launch was a highly ambitious project which deserved to succeed and was typical of the flamboyant style of the Fiat PR team at the time. The Uno Turbo was launched with a similar fanfare, but this time the company chose Rio de Janeiro and centred the launch around the Brazilian Grand Prix and Copacabana Beach – proof perhaps that racing cars can be relied upon more than space shuttles.

SNOW, SAND AND SUN

Swedish manufacturers have the advantage of being able to show off the cold-weather qualities of their cars because of their country's proximity to the Arctic. Volvo's choice of the Land of the Midnight Sun was quite an innovation for a new model launch, particularly when, instead of five-star hotels, they put journalists up in luxurious caravans.

The French Peugeot company became known as the king of the desert launches when they chose the Western Sahara and invited journalists to drive their new standard family saloon across that massive expanse of sand. Getting stuck was all part of the fun and the superb back-up team organized by Corrado Provera, the company's PR chief, made sure that they weren't stranded for long. It was certainly a new experience for most of the journalists and gave them something extra to write about.

FORD WIVES' TALES AND OTHERS

Ford of Britain was the first car company to invite the wives of motoring writers to accompany their husbands on new model launches. However, what should have been a good idea and money well spent, in view of the input which many women have on the choice of car, did create a few problems.

The first occasion was when Ford launched their new Capri hardback in Torquay. The wives were invited and at the end of the launch party everyone was given a large crystal vase to take home with them as a gift. On the eve of the official announcement the Ford PR department swung into action again and sent all the wives a magnificent bouquet of flowers, along with a message expressing the hope that they had enjoyed the time they spent with Ford testing the new Capri, to be announced the following morning.

This was all good PR stuff and typical of Ford efficiency. The only problem was that several of the motoring writers hadn't bothered to pass the company's invitation on to their wives and had taken their mistresses and girlfriends instead.

Wives were also invited to the Granada launch at Chewton Glen in Hampshire, but the Ford hospitality was too lavish for one of them, who drank far too much after dinner and retired to bed in a rather bad way. She managed to put in an appearance at breakfast the following morning, but was very sick when she accompanied her husband later on a test drive of the new Granada. Ford were obviously in a 'no win' situation when he slated the car in his newspaper report and put his wife's sickness down to the Granada's poor rear suspension and roadholding. Fortunately, all the other wives felt all right, so this particular report proved the exception amongst the accolades.

Perhaps it was fortunate that wives were not invited to the launch of the Mark I Cortina, or they would have come across the embarrassing sight of the company's Chief Engineer and Chief Development Engineer standing rather forlornly by the side of the Al, when their Cortina acquired a puncture and they didn't know how to jack the car up and change the wheel.

They had been following the road-test route between London and Stamford mapped out for the motoring journalists, and were due to join them for lunch at Burghley. Journalists can be kind, and nothing was written about their gaff, but the two senior engineers had to put up with a lot of ribbing from their own colleagues when they arrived late.

Ford took everyone to Morocco for the launch of the Mark I Escort in 1968, but the deserted desert roads proved too great a temptation for some of the journalists, including Courtenay Edwards, one of the most distinguished motoring writers of the postwar era. A lot of friendly rivalry went on between the top national motoring correspondents, several of whom decided to ignore the planned fuel stop and sped on into the desert.

When the Ford service truck came across them, standing by the roadside having run out of fuel, Courtenay Edwards gave the mechanic a big grin and said: "There was no way I was going to stop while I was in the lead."

The racing driver Innes Ireland took his labradors with him for the launch of the four-wheel-drive Sierra estate car in Scotland. He was chased by the police after exceeding the speed limit, but managed to open up such a gap between the Sierra and the patrol car that he was able to stop, unload the dogs, and walk with them some 50 yards back along the road before the police car came round the corner. They obviously couldn't believe that anyone could have driven so fast and got so far ahead of them so they ignored Innes and kept going.

In Cyprus, during the Sierra Sapphire launch in 1985, the test route instructions said everyone should turn right at George's bar. One of the motoring writers took it to be an official coffee stop and pulled in for some refreshments. When he found that he was alone he flagged down several of the following cars and insisted that they join him.

An hour later and after a substantial amount of food and drink had been consumed, he found that they had run up a considerable bill. His colleagues expected him to be the host and drove off, but unfortunately he didn't have enough money. He was saved by the arrival of the Ford service crew, who had seen the car and thought he may have had some sort of mechanical trouble. They were relieved to find it was only a cash problem and happily paid the bill.

Basil Cardew was a brilliant newspaperman as well as one of Fleet Street's most accomplished motoring correspondents for more than 40 years. He joined the *Daily Express* from the Press Association and covered every major motoring event for the paper, including races, rallies and record-breaking attempts, as well as all the new model launches.

The son of a well-known racing journalist, it was while he was with the

Press Association, where it was essential to be first with the news, that he learned some short cuts which he wasn't above using from time to time, in order to get an exclusive for his paper. His first motoring assignment for the Press Association was a race meeting at Brooklands. Malcolm Campbell crashed on the banking, badly damaging his car, but fortunately escaping with only minor cuts and bruises. Having learned that the great man was all right, but realizing that there would be little chance of an interview until he had received first aid treatment, he used his imagination and telephoned through to his office an interview with Malcolm Campbell, describing what it was like to crash on the Brooklands banking and escape death at 100mph.

Some time afterwards he asked a colleague the name of the tall man who was approaching them in greasy overalls with his arm in a sling and carrying a rather battered helmet. "That's Malcolm Cambell, the man you you are meant to have interviewed", came the surprised reply. Basil always enjoyed that story.

He did, however, manage to get his genuine exclusive when Ford launched the new 100E Anglia and Prefect in 1953. The company shipped one example of each to Paris for the motor show and they were held overnight for safe keeping in the Ford of France showroom in the *Champs Elysees*. Basil got to know of this and was quickly on the scene when the cars were due to be loaded onto a transporter for the onward journey. He helped push them across the showroom floor and then drove each car across the pavement and onto the transporter himself. The 30-yard journey at the wheel of the new Anglia and Prefect models was all he needed for a front-page story about his drive along the *Champs Elysees* with Ford's new wonder cars and the effect the new models had on the Paris taxi drivers, who doffed their caps in amazement. There will never be another Basil Cardew.

New model launches did sometimes get out of hand with some rather boisterous parties. During the Mark IV Zephyr Zodiac launch in Tunisia, Martyn Watkins of *Cars and Car Conversions* magazine insisted on dancing on a table. Unfortunately, he fell off and broke his ankle. After Martyn had been flown home for treatment, his doctor pointed out that the break was so bad and his ankle was in such a mess, that if he had remained in Tunisia he would probably have qualified to register there as a disabled beggar!

Using local entertainers in Middle Eastern countries can also present some unexpected problems, particularly when snakes are involved. During the Zephyr launch, Maurice Smith, the popular editor of *Autocar* magazine, was persuaded to join a snake charmer in his act, but became rather apprehensive when the man coiled a large, rather lethal-looking snake round his neck, to

the obvious delight of the audience, who gave them both a round of applause.

Unfortunately, when everybody clapped loudly the snake must have felt it was expected do something rather spectacular for an encore, so bit Maurice on the nose! In fact, it sank its fangs in so deeply that it was some time before its owner could persuade the snake to let go and they were able to stop the bleeding. Maurice returned home with the end of his nose covered in a large sticking plaster and an unexpected memento of the trip – a photograph someone had taken of the snake being prized from his nose by a rather worried snake charmer. Despite his efforts to keep a typically British stiff upper lip, the expression on Maurice's face could not belie his feelings about the act and his obvious loathing for snakes.

MR CORD AND AL CAPONE

The Chairman of the Cord Motor Company had a novel way of entertaining other motor company heads when they visited the private yacht he kept moored on Lake Michigan. After lunch he usually organized some clay pigeon shooting, but instead of shotguns everyone had to use the Thompson

submachine gun used in the infamous St Valentine's Day Massacre, when the American gangster Al Capone arranged for the members of a rival gang to be lined up against a garage wall and shot.

The weapon was so powerful and leaped about so much when it was fired that few of the guests managed to hit a clay, but they were able to boast that they had used Al Capone's murderous weapon in a shoot out!

SUCH DISLOYALTY

For nearly 70 years the British motor industry was very much a family affair. The cycle pioneers lived mainly in the Coventry area. They knew each other and their children grew up together. The families inter-married and the trend continued when the pioneer cycle manufacturers became the pioneer car makers.

When Billy and Reggie Rootes became motor manufacturers in Coventry they were faced with a family problem. They had provided jobs for several members of the family and didn't feel that Desmond Rootes, one of their stepbrothers, was matching up to the high standards they expected from all their senior executives.

It was eventually decided that he would have to go, but as he was a close member of the family, Billy felt that he should have the task of firing him and invited him to London so that they could lunch together at the Ritz. He thought that the news of his sacking would be less painful if it came after a couple of softening-up dry Martinis and a good lunch.

The waiter had just brought the menu when Desmond Rootes provided his own shock news. Taking a nerve-settling gulp from his dry Martini he said:

"I have been wondering how to tell you this Billy, but I want to leave Rootes. Lord Austin has offered me a job at a higher salary, which I have decided to accept."

"What's that?" Billy roared, to the obvious surprise of the people sitting at nearby tables. "You are planning to leave me and go to work for another motor company, and one of our major competitors as well? I won't hear of such disloyalty. You are staying with Rootes and I am increasing your salary."

Desmond remained with the Rootes Group for more than 30 years.

THE DEVIOUS SCHEMES OF CHARLIE MORRIS

The loyalty which Billy Rootes instilled in his personal staff was quite remarkable. His chauffeur George Vallet and his private secretary Linda Drury were both with him for more than 40 years and although Charlie Morris, his travelling secretary, was fired regularly for some misdemeanour or other, real or imaginary, Billy always wisely forgot about it the following morning and they remained together until he died.

Apart from being an excellent secretary and valet, Charlie Morris did have his faults which Billy always overlooked. He rather liked his roguish nature and knew that it would be difficult to find anyone who would be more loyal, efficient, work such long hours or put up with his outbursts. Morris had been employed by the Maharajah of Alwar, until he had been deposed by order of the Viceroy for misruling his state, misappropriating its funds and exercising his *roit de seigneur* over too many Indian girls. He may even have got away with all those malpractices had he not flown into a rage and tried to set fire to his polo pony after losing an important match. That was too much for the British Raj and proved his final undoing.

The time Morris spent in India gave him a taste for good living, and after he went to work for Billy Rootes he would sneak any whisky or brandy which was not locked away and often watered the gin to disguise the amount he had taken. He always marked the bottles, however, so that he would know which they were and make sure they weren't used in a dry Martini, where its weakened strength might be noticed.

I always knew if Morris had been watering the gin whenever Billy invited me to help myself to a dry Martini at his Mayfair home and Morris was there with some letters for him to sign. He always rushed forward to help with the drinks in case I picked up the wrong gin bottle.

Morris travelled the world with Billy, organizing all his travelling arrangements and hotel accommodation and settling the bills, but he was not above impersonating his famous employer when he'd met a girl he wanted to impress.

Billy's son Brian and I caught him out one evening in Paris, when we were having a drink in the bar of one of the more exclusive restaurants while we decided whether to stay for dinner. When we sent for the menu the head waiter came across and asked whether we would be joining Lord Rootes at his table, as he had already booked. This came as rather a surprise as we knew that Billy Rootes had flown to America that evening and left Morris to pack and return to London the following day.

We told the waiter that we would be going elsewhere for dinner, but as soon as he was out of earshot Brian turned to me and said:

"I'll bet Charlie Morris is up to his old tricks again and having a night out using my father's name. He's probably got some young French girl he wants to impress. Let's wait and see."

We didn't have long to wait. A few minutes later Morris arrived, wearing one of Lord Rootes' dinner jackets and accompanied by an attractive blonde. They were ushered to one of the best tables in the window and judging by the attention they were receiving the name Lord Rootes was already having the desired effect.

On our way out Brian walked up to their table with a big grin on his face and said:

"Hello Lord Rootes. What a surprise to see you here tonight, I hope you have a pleasant evening."

Brian chuckled to himself as we left Billy's rather red-faced secretary and said:

"I'll bet Charlie Morris will have more than sex on his mind tonight."

AN EXPENSIVE BRANDY

Brian Rootes' sense of fun cost us dearly when we were on our way back from a new car launch in the South of France accompanied by a group of motoring writers. Because there was little time during our busy schedule for them to do any personal shopping, we had arranged for everyone to be given a bottle of brandy and an expensive bottle of perfume as a gift. To ensure that there wouldn't be any problem when we arrived at London Airport we had told the customs officials, who agreed for everyone to pass through customs control without being stopped.

Everything would have gone smoothly had we not been held up in Paris and spent several frustrating hours in the airport bar. Brian spent some time trying to buy a massive bottle of brandy which was on special display. It was far too big to carry and had its own basket mounted on wheels and with a walking stick handle so that it could be pushed along. He eventually got his way and bought the brandy as a gift for his father-in-law, whose birthday he had forgotten.

Everybody was quite merry by the time we landed at London Airport and Brian led the way through customs, proudly wheeling his massive bottle of brandy. The customs officers, who were ready to wave us through, immediately pounced. Everyone was searched and unfortunately many of our party had bought expensive gifts at the Paris Duty Free Shop while we were waiting, and were taxed heavily as a result. As Brian's bottle of brandy had caused the problem, we felt honour-bound to settle everyone's bill. That must have been the most expensive bottle of brandy he ever bought.

AN UPWARDS BUILD

When Rootes bought Singer the company had what must have been the world's only vertical car assembly line. Stocks of chassis were kept on the third floor, above the offices, and as each car was being assembled it was swung out through the window at the end of the line, then hauled in through another on the floor above.

Assembly workers were paid danger money to turn each car round before it reached the next floor level, so that it was facing the right way. The process was repeated until the final assembly on the top floor, when the completed cars were taken down to ground level for testing.

Singer was the company where Billy Rootes had started as a penny-an-hour apprentice and selling Singer cars had set him up in business. The two foremen he used to make tea for before the First World War were still there and so was the lathe he used to use. His old workmates were immediately retired on good pensions and the lathe was placed in the Rootes museum. Singer production was moved to the Rootes Ryton-on-Dunsmore plant in Coventry.

The building housing the vertical assembly line was turned into a modern stores depot.

TESTING TIMES

Road-test reports are an essential feature of every new model announcement. Manufacturers tell the public only what they would like them to know about a car in their advertisements, but road-test reports are the work of individual journalists, who should be obliged to tell their readers the truth. There is little point in not providing cars for them to write about, because advertisements may give a false impression of a new model's performance, or lack of it; once the car gets in the hands of the discerning public, the cat is quickly out of the bag, and the correspondence columns can become filled with letters from irate owners complaining that they have been misled.

Although those writing the road-test reports are free to comment on quality, performance and appearance, the manufacturers should at least be able to ensure that the cars being tested have all been properly serviced and are in excellent condition. Unfortunately, this doesn't always happen.

The first car that I road-tested was the new Morris Oxford, but I hadn't been told that a rear wing had been dented during the previous road-test and the manufacturer hadn't been able to repair the damage before delivering the car to me that weekend. I was out when their driver arrived and left the keys with the commissionaire, and it was dark by the time I collected the Morris Oxford from the office car park later that evening.

I didn't notice the dent until the following morning and presumed that the damage must have occurred either while it was in the office car park or outside my block of flats during the night. I felt responsible and rather than return my first road-test car with a dent, I telephoned Frank Grounds, who had a successful transport business, and he agreed to have the dent filled and the wing resprayed that same day. He was a member of the Ford rally team and we had become friends during the first postwar RAC Rally when I was driving a Jaguar XK120. I returned the test car to the Morris Company's headquarters at Cowley on the Monday, but as soon as I arrived the Public Relations Manager apologized about the dent.

"There wasn't enough time to have it fixed without cancelling the test and so I hope you didn't mind about the small dent in the wing."

"Not a bit", I replied, but I didn't want to risk the dent being seen on any of the photographs we took and so I had it repaired."

The look of surprise on his face was worth the cost!

I don't know whether there is such a thing as an unlucky car, but when Ford loaned me one of their new Consuls to road-test for my newspaper, I came close to writing it off when my wife and I were returning home from Warwickshire. As we were approaching Northolt Airport the driver of a Morris Minor suddenly pulled across into the fast lane while I was overtaking and attempted to make a U-turn to cross over to the other carriageway. I braked hard and tried to miss him, but a collision was unavoidable. The impact turned the Consul over and we slid along with my right ear only inches from the road, with safety glass from the windscreen being sprayed inside my shirt. When I took it off that evening, glass dropped onto the carpet like confetti.

It says a great deal for the strength and design of the Consul that my wife and I escaped with only a few cuts and bruises. The driver of the other car, who admitted that he hadn't seen the Consul in his mirror when he went to turn right, was completely unscathed. He explained that he was on a visit to Britain and became lost. He was trying to turn back along the dual carriageway when he saw me at the last minute.

Ford told me that the Consul had only just been repaired after being smashed up while it was on loan to Donald Campbell. Basil Cardew had it after me and managed to write it off completely. That must surely have been an unlucky car.

My luck was certainly in when I was on my way to Silverstone to test one of the Jowett Jupiter Le Mans team cars. A Jupiter, driven by Tommy Wise and Tommy Wisdom, had won the 1½-litre class at the Le Mans 24-Hours race in France in 1950 and, encouraged by that success, Jowett entered a team of three cars the following year. They again won the 1½-litre class, but this time it was the car driven by Marcel Becquart and Gordon Wilkins which was successful, although Tommy Wisdom's lap of 80.60mph was the fastest in the class.

After the second Jowett success, jovial John Baldwin, the company's popular Publicity Manager, invited me to test one of the team cars and I jumped at the chance. I collected the Jupiter from the company's London headquarters in Albemarle Street, and before I set off for Silverstone, John warned me: "For goodness sake keep out of trouble and don't get stopped with all that high-octane fuel on board. You mustn't use ordinary petrol, but there are enough cans of racing fuel behind the front seats and in the boot to get you there and back". It was all rather illegal, but we seemed willing to take a lot of foolish chances in those days.

I thought it best to keep to the minor roads, but had only reached as far as St John's Wood when the driver of a rather battered Standard shot the lights and hit the Jupiter behind the driver's seat. I didn't hesitate, but jumped from the car and ran, in case the cans split, the high-octane fuel caught fire and the car blew up. Shoppers who heard the crash and saw me running away must have thought that I was a hit-and-run driver. They weren't to know that the car I was running from was more like a miniature petrol bowser.

With the force of the impact it was surprising that none of the cans broke open, spilling their contents, particularly as several had been dented. By the time I returned to the Jupiter a small crowd had begun to gather and I felt it wise to get it out of harm's way as soon as possible.

With the help of the rather crestfallen driver of the other car and some onlookers, the damaged vehicle was pushed into the comparative safety of a side street. The Standard driver seemed as keen as I was not to involve the police and agreed to stand guard while I telephoned for help and arranged for a local garage to tow the Jupiter away. I learned later that the Standard wasn't insured and that was why he had been so keen not to cause any trouble.

His luck was in as well because Jowett certainly didn't want to make any claim against him in view of the rather dodgy situation with all the illegal cans of fuel. When I telephoned John Baldwin and told him what had happened there was a moment's pause, then he said:

"I'll bet you could do with a drink. Jump in a cab and meet me at the Ritz. A stiff drink and a spot of lunch and you will soon feel better. Look on the bright side. If those cans had exploded we'd probably both have been for the high jump."

How right he was!

John Baldwin was a true public relations professional who later joined Rover. I was delighted when Marcel Becquart and Gordon Wilkins won the 1½-litre class for Jowett again in 1952 and on that occasion I was able to give the company some well-deserved publicity. I decided, however, not to test drive any of the team cars, just in case I had used up all my luck.

During the time that I was head of public relations for the Rootes Group, we kept fleets of road-test cars in London and Scotland for use by the press. The cars were always kept in excellent condition, but even so there were a few occasions when things went wrong.

When the new Humber Super Snipe was sent to the motoring editor of one national newspaper, he wrote a glowing report about every feature of the car, except for the steering, which he said was rather heavy and not very positive. When it was checked, we found that the wheels were out of alignment. The driver did then admit that he had hit a high kerb very hard when the Super Snipe was being delivered, but had hoped that his mistake wouldn't be noticed.

When I rang to explain the reason for the problems with the steering, back came the perfect reply:

"I thought there must have been something wrong, but it is such a lovely car, the steering was the only thing I could find fault with. If I hadn't criticized something, my readers wouldn't have believed all the nice things I said about the Humber and so you should really be pleased."

There are occasions when winning can be very difficult.

Fortunately, considering the thousands of miles covered by road-test cars each year, it is quite rare for one to be written off, or even damaged, but when a Yorkshire journalist crashed a brand-new Sunbeam while he was test-driving it near Aberdeen, he really did us a good turn, although I didn't think so at the time.

A notoriously dangerous bend before a narrow bridge proved his undoing: he approached the bend far too quickly and the car crashed through a hedge at speed before rolling over and over down a steep embankment and ending upside down in a field. He and his passenger were lucky to escape with only a few cuts and bruises, but the car was damaged beyond repair.

As the driver had been drinking rather heavily that lunch time, I was rather annoyed at the way in which the Sunbeam had been written off, leaving our press fleet a car short. The following morning, however, I had a telephone call from the Engineering Director in Coventry, asking if I would let him have the crashed Sunbeam if he replaced it with a new one.

I thought at first that he must have lost his marbles, until he explained that they needed the results of a roll-over test as part of an extensive crash test programme they had to complete before the Sunbeam could be be sold in America. He and his colleagues had planned to use dummies and crash a car by remote control, but the Sunbeam which the journalist had crashed so impressively would give them all the measurements and other information they needed, without having to set up any special tests.

I was happy to arrange the exchange and forgive the guilty driver his lapse, which hadn't been so unfortunate after all.

When *Autocar* magazine wrote off a new Hillman Minx convertible, fortunately without injury to anyone except the driver's pride, the accident was more like a scene from an old Buster Keaton movie. The Motor Industry Research Association's new research and development establishment near Nuneaton had just been opened, and the magazine, which always tested every new car very thoroughly, had been given permission to make use of the extensive facilities available there. The *Autocar*'s test team was nearing the end of their programme and had left the water splash until last. The plan was to drive the Hillman Minx convertible at speed through the water splash, which was several inches deep, to test whether or not the underside of the car was waterproof.

The driver unfortunately mistook the water test used for checking tanks and other military vehicles, which was several feet deep, for the water splash used for cars, which was only a few inches deep. He realized his mistake too late, when the white convertible with red upholstery sank to the

bottom of the tank in several feet of water and he was forced to swim to safety. By the time the Hillman was pulled clear, its upholstery, carpets and interior instrumentation had become a soggy mess and the car had to be stripped down completely and rebuilt. The unfortunate driver also took some time to dry out.

PLENTY OF BOUNCE

The Morgan sportscar is one of the outstanding success stories in the 100-year history of the British motor industry. The remarkable three-wheeler, produced by H F S Morgan when he started the company, was the first light car to develop the same sporting image as a motorcycle.

The big V-twin cylinder JAP or Anzani engine, positioned between the two front wheels to catch as much air as possible, drove the single wheel at the back by means of a shaft and chains.

To prove how sporty the new three-wheelers were, Morgan and his young wife decided to take part in the driving trials which were becoming very popular, but to begin with they had difficulty in keeping the single rear driving wheel of their vehicle in contact with the ground when they had to

tackle a steep incline or a particularly muddy hill.

They found that the best solution was to try to bounce up and down together, but this proved a tricky art to master when the driver was having to steer, change gear and use the accelerator all at the same time. However, they succeeded more often than not, gaining many victories. Morgan's pretty wife always had plenty of admirers among the spectators who went along especially to watch her bouncing up and down, keeping time with her husband, while their sporty little three-wheeler made its ascent.

ALL MAPPED OUT

Having to compete in an international rally without the proper maps must be every rally driver's nightmare, but it can occur, even with a works entry.

It happened to me when I was driving a works Sunbeam-Talbot 90 in the RAC Rally with Charles Fothergill. We were starting from Scarborough and as he was held up on a story and would be late leaving Fleet Street, I collected our car from Coventry. In return he agreed to look after all the paperwork and mark up the maps we needed, particularly the ones for the mountain sections.

After an excellent dinner that evening at the Grand Hotel run by Frank Laughton, the brother of the actor Charles Laughton, we joined Tommy Wisdom and Lord Selsdon in their room for a nightcap and to go over the following day's route with them. Charles went to get our maps and returned with the news that he must have left them on his desk at the office. I didn't know whether to laugh or cry. We were heading for Scotland the following day and had to leave before the shops were open.

This didn't seem to deter Charles, who ordered another bottle of brandy and announced that he would fix everything the next morning. It turned out to be wishful thinking on his part: the only shop open was the local newsagent and the only maps he had were sixpenny cyclist's maps.

Like condemned men we ate a hearty breakfast and to everyone's amusement, particularly Tommy Wisdom's, set off for the Highlands with our cyclist's map and Charles doing the navigating. After a while he even suggested that with his hangover a cyclist's map was much easier to follow and leaving the other maps behind in London might prove to be a blessing in disguise.

As it turned out he was probably right. We didn't lose our way once, but Tommy Wisdom and Lord Selsdon, driving one of the new Jaguars, threw away their chances of success when they took the wrong road and ended the rally with time penalties. They were also no longer on speaking terms.

After my experience I knew how Peter Harper must have felt in the Tulip Rally, having got his first works drive with the Sunbeam-Talbot team when John Cutts, his very experienced codriver, suddenly announced that he had left all their specially marked-up maps in his office at Rootes. At least they possessed a Michelin map of Europe, but any real chance they had of victory had been left sitting on a desk in Coventry. Peter Harper did become a very successful works driver and a worthy rally champion.

Tommy Wisdom was driving the new Mark II Sunbeam-Talbot 90 with David Humphrey and Tony Phillips in the 1951 Monte Carlo Rally and rather fancied his chances. They were doing well and still in contention when they reached Monte Carlo, but Tommy was annoyed to find that on the final speed trial taking place the following day in the mountains overlooking the town, they were due to start just behind Mike Couper and Lord Selsdon. He knew they were not really interested in winning the rally, but had entered a rather grand Daimler fitted out with every conceivable luxury device, with the intention of winning that year's *Concours d'Elegance*.

Having had his usual bottle of champagne, Tommy sought out Lord Selsdon in the bar later that evening, tapped him on the shoulder, then putting his monacle to his eye said:

"My Lord, if you and Mike Couper are hoping to win any fancy prizes in this rally, let me make one thing clear. When we catch up with you on the mountain circuit tomorrow, you'd better not hold us up, or that bloody barge of yours won't be in any fit state to take part in the concours! Good night."

Then he let the monacle drop from his eye, bowed to his lordship and walked slowly out of the bar in the direction of the stairs.

His wife Bill was also a fine racing driver and a successful rally driver. When she was joined up with Sheila Van Damm they made a very formidable team in more ways than one, Bill Wisdom being slightly built whereas Sheila was rather sturdy.

Her considerable strength came in useful, however, in their first Monte

Carlo rally together, when they were in a Hillman Minx JWK 459, known in the Rootes team as 'Old Faithful'. They suffered a puncture in the Alps and the jack broke as they were changing the wheel. Without a moment's hesitation, Sheila lifted the car clear of the ground and held it there while Bill Wisdom fitted the spare wheel!

Sheila was always known as 'Sloshy' in the team because of her liking for champagne cocktails, but she was a tough competitor. She became the European Women's Rally Champion and won her class in the gruelling *Mille Miglia* road race in Italy, driving a modified Sunbeam Rapier.

A BARON, A BEAR AND A WHITE RAT

The motor industry has never been short of characters and Baron Rolf Beck, the Czechoslovakian-born industrialist and Chairman of the Slip Group, was among the most colourful. After being brought up on the family estate at Rohow he went to Theresanium Military Academy and then spent some time at universities in Geneva, Zurich and Vienna, where he gained several scientific and engineering degrees. He then became one of Europe's best known playboys, spending much of his time sailing and skiing, usually in the company of beautiful women, and racing motor cars.

Rolf Beck had become a successful amateur racing driver when the Skoda arms firm suggested that he should help them to become established in Britain and start manufacturing Skoda cars there using 51 per cent British parts, with the other 49 per cent imported from Czechoslovakia. Hitler upset their plans, but the baron found he liked living in Britain and formed his own company here in 1939 to make and sell oil and petrol additives. He chose the name Slip because it was easy to pronounce in any language.

During the war he worked for Rolls-Royce and the British Government, but as soon as the war ended he set about building up his own Slip Group. He toured the world promoting his own methods of saving oil, based on the theory that the crude oil being produced by most of the world's new oilfields contained too much sulphur. He claimed that his chemical formula not only dealt with the problem, but also reduced engine wear and allowed more power to be generated.

He married a Scottish girl and bought Layham Hall, a country estate in Norfolk. His Slip Group prospered and Rolf Beck's stocky figure became a familiar sight at motor shows, race meetings and other motoring events. The papers referred to him as the 'Roving Baron', because of his frequent business trips abroad, when he was usually accompanied by one of his beautiful mistresses. He married three times and the third occasion was in 1990, not long before he died aged 77.

He was still married to his first wife, Elizabeth, when we first met and he asked me to became his company's public relations consultant. I found out later that my father had been one of his first clients and helped him get started.

It may have been because Rolf was away so much that Elizabeth kept a menagerie of exotic pets, but I didn't know this when I accepted an invitation to visit their country estate. Rolf sent his car to meet me at the station and I was impressed by the professional way in which his chauffeur, cap under arm, held the door open and saw me comfortably settled before we drove off. The journey didn't take long, but when we arrived at Layham Hall the chauffeur's behaviour was very different. He didn't get out of the car, but pointed to the door bell. Before I could ring it, however, he and the car had disappeared out of sight.

The maid who answered the bell closed the door quickly behind me and led the way through to the study, before letting the baron know that I had arrived. I began to understand the chauffeur's strange behaviour and the speed with which the maid closed the front door, when I walked across to the window. A large shaggy bear ambled across the lawn and stared into the room at me before wandering off down the path. As he did so the study door opened and Rolf appeared carrying a cricket bat which he leant against the wall.

"I didn't know you played cricket," I said, as we shook hands.

He gave me a broad grin:

"I don't. I hate the game. The bat belongs to my son, but I carry it as protection against Yogi bear."

I told him that I had already seen the animal wandering around the garden. Rolf shook his head:

"It should be kept locked up, but my wife won't hear of it. The damn thing is allowed to wander all over the place. It used to follow her when she went out riding, until people in the village complained. I had to shoot the previous one she had here when it went berserk and attacked her. Whatever you do, stay in the house while Yogi is on the loose."

I made a mental note to make sure that all our future meetings were held in London, especially after Rolf's wife had insisted during lunch that this five-foot Malayan sun bear was not only "perfectly sweet" to have wandering loose about the place, but also "such fun to roll about with and take for walks". However, she did seem to weaken her argument by adding, "Of course, he is so huge and has such enormous claws that he could quite easily destroy you".

I was not surprised to learn that a few weeks later it had run amok through the house, causing several hundred pounds worth of damage and been promptly despatched to a zoo at Cromer. It was, perhaps, fortunate that Rolf was away at the time, or Yogi might have received the same fate as the previous bear.

Despite his size, I preferred the bear to some of the other strange pets the baroness kept, including the large white rat which shared her bed when Rolf was away. She knew about his mistresses, and replacing him with a white rat when he was abroad with one of them, may have been her way of showing him how she felt.

My first encounter with the rat took place in their London flat. Elizabeth Beck was a close friend of Joy Adamson, who had achieved fame through her successful books and the film about the lioness Elsa and her cubs. I agreed to help publicize Joy's latest book and took the editor of the *News of the World* for drinks with them one evening.

I went into the dining room at the flat to telephone my wife and as she answered the phone a large rat ran along the sideboard and began sniffing at my half empty glass of champagne.

What wife wouldn't be concerned to be told that her husband would be late for dinner and was sharing a glass of champagne with a large white rat. Her suggestion that I should leave my car in London and get a taxi home immediately, also seemed like a good idea.

Elizabeth, however, was overjoyed when I told her about the rat in the dining room. It had, she explained, escaped from her bedroom and been hiding somewhere in her flat. It was perched on her shoulder, cleaning its whiskers, as I made my apologies and left.

THE HOBGOBLIN'S REVENGE?

John Zachary de Lorean and his wife Christina had been voted America's most glamorous couple: he was the swashbuckling wizzkid of General Motors who had started the American craze for large powerful cars and had doubled Pontiac's share of the home market in just 10 years; she was Ferrare, the glamorous model who was featured on the covers of all the top fashion magazines.

The smooth-talking American automobile executive persuaded the British Government to spend £85 million on a factory in Ulster to build his revolutionary new gull-winged sportscar. It turned out to be the world's most disastrous sportscar venture and became a story involving deception, financial irregularities, false accounting, tax evasion and even drug smuggling – a feat unequalled during a century of car production on both sides of the Atlantic.

There are some, however, who insist that the venture was really doomed from the start, when some greedy workmen, foolishly tempted by a $100 note, had caused the displeasure of Ireland's famous 'little people'. The site chosen for the factory had been a 56-acre green field on the outskirts of Belfast. It had two streams running through it and a tree in the centre, exactly where the factory was due to be built.

The local workmen refused to cut down the tree, because of local folklore, but when the contractors let it be known one day that there was a $100 note hidden under its roots, it mysteriously disappeared during the night and the building was able to go ahead.

Those who know about such matters, however, still insist that the project's failure was really the work of the hobgoblins, who were angry at the loss of their tree and the streams where they used to play.

TOO MANY BALLS IN THE AIR

Three of the men involved in the De Lorean sportscar project had been colleagues of mine at Chrysler. The Chief Executive was Eugene Cafiero, a former President of Chrysler Corporation; the Financial Director was Joe Daly and the Managing Director was Don Lander, a tough, fast-talking Canadian, who'd been head of Chrysler Europe.

There was a lot to like about Don Lander, but his American management methods and insatiable zest for hard work didn't always go down well, particularly with some of the dealers who had worked with the Rootes brothers for many years. One of them was a charming Scot called Anderson, who was tall, rather gaunt and had a wonderfully dry sense of humour.

When I visited his company's stand at the Scottish motor show one year he suddenly asked me,

"What do you think of the wee man Lander?"

"I rather like him," I admitted, "he is certainly a workaholic and dedicated to his job."

"Aye, he is that. I've never known a man with so many balls in the air at the same time. The problem is, I have a distinct feeling at the moment that two of them are mine!"

A FISHY DEAL AND OPEN ALL HOURS

Selling cars is not always a straightforward business, but there cannot have been a fishier deal than the one done by Billy Rootes during the Fifties. He fully deserved the title of Britain's super salesman and when the Norwegian Government was so short of foreign currency that they imposed a strict quota system on all car imports, he proposed a barter deal and sold them extra Hillmans in exchange for fish, which they had in abundance.

I had never heard of Norwegian sild until he told me that we now had some 50 million of them, all neatly packed in tins and worth more than 3 million Kroner – 50,000 cases of which were waiting to be shipped to Britain. My colleagues and I were given the task of making the fish known to British housewives so that Rootes would be able to get a better price from the fish importers and distributors.

My research revealed that sild had been sold in Britain before the war in quite large quantities. The fish was similar in size to a sardine, but persuading British housewives to change their postwar buying habits was not going to be easy.

Selling fish certainly made a change from promoting cars, and we must have been reasonably successful because sild did become very popular. In fact, tins of them are still being sold in British supermarkets today.

Billy Rootes' arrival back in Britain from his frequent trips to America was usually followed by an intensive period of action by the company's sales staff, who were expected to try out many of the latest sales techniques he had seen in use over there. Not all were successful, however, particularly the idea he had for keeping the company's Piccadilly showrooms at Devonshire House open 24 hours a day.

He thought that would enable people coming into London's West End during the evening, for dinner or to see a show, to have an opportunity of wandering round the showrooms afterwards at their leisure and talking to the sales staff. There were also those whose jobs kept them in London at night who might like to visit the showrooms on their way home.

The idea had some merit, but it would have been costly and difficult to administer and was viewed with a considerable amount of alarm by the other members of the board who wondered whether there was a sufficient number of insomniacs in London to make it worthwhile.

It was one of the rare occasions when Billy Rootes didn't get his own way and it obviously wrangled with him. I thought he had forgotten about the idea until some weeks later when we were returning from a dinner at the Savoy Hotel and driving past the showrooms about midnight. A man in evening dress was leaning against the building and certainly seemed to be peering through the window at one of the cars. Billy shouted to his chauffeur to stop the car, and turning to me said:

"What have I been saying? That man's a potential customer. Go and let him into the showroom and see if you can sell him a car. If you can we'll have just the evidence I need to prove me right."

I rang the bell for the caretaker, but it was quite obvious that the purchase of a new car was not what the man had in mind. He was standing cross-legged and obviously in some discomfort. As soon as Jimmy, the night watchman, opened the door I signalled to the man to follow me and pointed to the sign on the door of the gentleman's loo in the showroom. With a grateful nod he disappeared inside and emerged a few minutes later with a look of relief on his face.

A proper salesman might have succeeded where I failed, but I felt rather stupid asking whether he was interested in any of the gleaming new cars on show. Although Billy Rootes' potential customer obviously thought I was pulling his leg, he did explain that he was already a Humber owner and had recently purchased a new Hillman Minx for his wife. Apparently, he was visiting London to attend a regimental reunion and had decided to walk off the effects of a good dinner and far more wine than he would normally drink. Unfortunately, his hotel was further away than he had thought and by the time he reached Devonshire House he realized that he couldn't go any further. His last words as we shook hands and he set off at a brisk pace towards Park Lane were:

"I'll never forget Rootes and you for what you did. You and Lord Rootes can rest assured that when the time comes to change my car I will be buying another Humber."

Lord Rootes gave me a searching look as we drove off:

"That didn't take long. Did you sell him a car?"

"Afraid not" I replied, "but at least we now know we have one satisfied customer."

He didn't look amused.

A NICE LITTLE EARNER

Although Lord Rootes never managed to put his 'Open All Hours' policy into effect, the Rootes Halkin House showrooms and service station in Halkin Street, at the end of Piccadilly, did do a brisk trade at night during one period, because of the entrepreneurial activities of one of the company's petrol pump attendants – although none of the profit went to Rootes. It was only by chance that I learned that the building was being used as a brothel and had become "a nice little earner" at night.

I was leaving for a lunch appointment when the receptionist at Devonshire House told me that a young man had arrived who was very anxious to speak to me about a rather delicate matter which he didn't want to discuss with anyone else. He turned out to be a second lieutenant in the army, who had come to London with a colleague to celebrate getting their commissions. The previous evening, after going to a club and having rather too much to drink, they had been picked up by a couple of prostitutes who took them by taxi to Halkin House. Money changed hands and the petrol pump attendant let them into the building. They were offered the choice of using the large leather couches in the reception area, or the luxurious rear seats of the ambassadorial Humbers which were parked ovenight in the garage alongside. It was obvious that the girls knew their way around the building and that they weren't the only ones making use of the facilities.

My informant assured me that he wasn't looking for any payment for the information and turned down my offer to settle his hotel bill, or to compensate him for any out of pocket expenses. He was obviously very embarrassed about the incident, so much so that I couldn't help wondering why he had come to see me. He must have read my thoughts, explaining that his father had a business in Manchester and if his premises were being used for immoral purposes at night, he hoped that someone would also tell him about it. The young lieutenant left to catch his train without even telling me his name and I felt it wiser not to ask.

Although Billy Rootes always encouraged private enterprise, this was a business venture which needed nipping in the bud as soon as possible. So, I went to see John Routly, our company secretary, who was a lawyer and should, I felt, know the best way of tackling the problem. As I explained what had happened we both saw the funny aspects of the situation and thought of the possible headlines if the newspapers got to hear of it: 'Rootes' house of ill-repute forced to close'; 'Brothel most successful area of Rootes' business'; or perhaps 'Lord Rootes' new open-all-hours policy proves successful'.

Secrecy was important and we employed a private detective to keep watch on the Halkin Street premises. He had no difficulty in catching the petrol pump attendant and his team of prostitutes redhanded, but we decided not to prosecute. The last thing we wanted was publicity and the ambassadors would have been very upset to have learned what went on in the back of their official cars at night. The attendant was fired, the locks on the entrance to the building were changed, and few people were any the wiser. It was, however, the only time when a Rootes showroom was 'Open All Hours'.

THE AVENGERS INVADE MALTA

Car companies are often criticized for launching their new models at expensive overseas venues instead of at British resorts, but can you really blame them? It has probably taken their design team three or four years, at a cost of many millions of pounds, to produce a new model which they hope will appeal to press and public alike, and bring their company success and prosperity for several years to come. With British weather usually as unpredictable in advance as a national lottery, even during the summer months, they certainly wouldn't want first impressions of their new car to be gained during a drive in the drizzle at Brighton.

There is also the question of security. Motoring writers are usually given an opportunity to try a new model several weeks before the announcement date, with a promise that they will hold up publication of their reports until then, but they couldn't be expected to do so if the car had already been seen and possibly photographed by thousands of British holidaymakers.

During the late Sixties and early Seventies, the Government's foreign currency restrictions put paid to all those exotic places in the sun that we usually chose for the press to test our latest new model. Therefore, we had to look around for somewhere in the Sterling area. Chrysler was ready to launch the Avenger towards the end of 1969, but it was decided that a further three months of intensive testing was needed, so the launch was postponed until February 1970. The Avenger was a particularly interesting new car to many of us who had been involved with the Rootes brothers and held them in high regard, because it was the last model they planned together before their brilliant partnership came to an end with Billy Rootes' death in 1964. Chrysler now controlled the destiny of Rootes and the Avenger was the first entirely new model since the takeover. It was essential that the launch and the car should both prove to be a success.

Everyone in Britain and America knew the name Avenger, because of the very successful television series, with the bowler-hatted John Steed and his lovely assistants doing battle with various villains each week, and so we planned to exploit the Avenger theme as much as possible in the launch.

Even if we had wanted to, there was no point in our trying to hold the press and dealer launches in Britain. February was a high-risk month for bad weather and even snow and we couldn't take the chance. We pleaded with the Government to allow us to have enough foreign currency to launch the car in North Africa, or some other warm climate, but they dug their toes in and refused point blank.

The only place within the Sterling area with a stable political situation and where there were enough good hotels with large conference rooms, adequate facilities for testing the cars, a good airport to enable journalists and dealers to be flown in and out easily, which could also offer a reasonable chance of good weather, seemed to be Malta. As soon as the announcement date was fixed, my colleague Bill Elsey and I flew there on a 24-hour fact-finding mission so that a final decision could be made that week, but our plane developed engine trouble on the way out and we were forced to spend 10 of the 24 hours we had been given in Naples.

This seemed at first like a bad omen. The old adage: 'See Naples and die' did cross our minds, but we cheered up when a fellow passenger turned out to be the Marketing Director of British European Airways, who made sure that we were booked into the best hotel and then gave us a slap-up dinner and a tour of the nightspots at the airline's expense.

We took the first plane to Malta in the morning, and despite our self-inflicted lack of sleep, worked all day and the following night in order to complete our investigation on time, catching the 5.30am plane back to London and writing our report during the flight.

Malta wasn't really the ideal place for a new car launch because of the island's 40mph speed limit, but we were encouraged by everyone's enthusiasm and willingness to co-operate, including the Governor. Before we left, Bill and I booked the three main hotels and persuaded the manager of the Malta Hilton to allow us to arrange for one of his ballroom walls to be knocked down, as well as some other structural alterations, which included building an additional display and entertaining area in the hotel's gazebo area by the swimming pool. We planned to arrange a major spectacular at the hotel, based on the Avenger theme, for the unveiling of the new car and every inch of space would be needed.

There were plenty of rough, hilly, winding roads on the island and we hired a disused airfield, where there weren't any speed restrictions, so that we could arrange speed and manoeuvrability tests. The hangars could also be turned into useful workshops for our mechanics and provide storage space for the 100 or so cars we would need. What we didn't know until later, although the lack of birds and wildlife on the island should have been a warning sign, was that many of the locals spent their spare time taking pot-shots at almost anything that moved, and the airfield was one of their favourite shooting grounds. We didn't want to upset the locals, but neither did we want to run the risk of any of our cars or guests being peppered with buckshot. I expressed our concern to Malta's Chief of Police and he made sure that the airfield was placed out of bounds to anyone with a gun for the duration of our stay there.

A fleet of transport planes were chartered to fly cars, spares and other equipment to the island. Crates for all the special film and sound equipment needed for the spectacular were tailor-made to fit the loading hatches of the transport planes, but there was a last-minute panic when the thicker prongs of the forklift trucks at Malta airport wouldn't fit the loading pallets, and valuable time was lost while each crate had to be manhandled off the aircraft.

When everything was ready charter planes flew a shuttle service between London and Malta, transporting the hundreds of British and foreign journalists, dealers and their wives, and the 14 different television crews, who were our guests during the three-week period of the launch. Ted Ray, John Le Mesurier, Lionel Blair, Ami Macdonald and a talented group of dancers were on the first plane and they stayed with us on the island to entertain the guests each evening.

The Avenger launch exceeded everyone's expectations and was acknowledged to be one of the most successful new car functions since the war. Thousands of column inches were written about the car and its performance and it was featured on scores of radio and television programmes, including the BBC's flagship *Panorama*, which had previously been very critical of the British motor industry.

Because so many of my colleagues and our guests came down to breakfast with hangovers each morning, I arranged for sparkling mineral water to be served with the meal. When Perrier water is served in a crystal glass it can look rather like 'bubbly' in a photograph or on film and the *Panorama* script writer, accidentally or on purpose, referred to us serving everybody champagne each morning at breakfast. Either way it didn't matter, because it did turn out to be a real champagne launch as far as we were concerned.

Due to all the publicity generated by the Malta function, the Avenger enabled Chrysler to double its market penetration in Britain in less than four months and more than a million of them were sold worldwide, in some form or another, between 1970 and 1981. Billy Rootes would have been delighted at its success.

OVER THE TOP

The new Avenger was due to make its first public appearance at the Geneva motor show. Chrysler had arranged for a number of cars to be sent from England to be tested throughout the show by foreign motoring journalists who had been unable to be in Malta. The worldwide publicity generated by

the Malta launch had already made the Avenger one of the most talked about models going on show for the first time at Geneva.

The cars for the Chrysler stand were sent by transporter, but as they were already registered and run-in, the dozen or so to be used for the road-test programme were driven there across Europe by a group of delivery drivers. Each driver had been carefully selected by the delivery company because of his ability and experience of driving on the Continent.

Many motoring journalists also drive to Geneva each year, using the visit as a good opportunity to try one of the new models sent to them for road-test and write about their journey. Those that did on that occasion had an unexpected bonus as they drove through France, when they suddenly came across one of the new Avengers, which had left the road on a particularly tight mountain bend and was resting in the branches of a tree below.

The car's driver was 'Mort' Morris-Goodall, who had been a well-known racing driver and drove an Aston Martin at Le Mans. Fortunately, he escaped serious injury, but Chrysler couldn't escape the bad publicity. Photographs of their much-vaunted new model perching rather ignominiously in the branches of a French tree, was hardly the image they were trying to portray to the world of a car with outstanding brakes and steering!

A REALLY HONEST INQUIRY

Salesmen on the motor company stands during motor show time must breathe a sigh of relief when the final day arrives. The dust raised by thousands of feet tramping down the aisles each day will probably have given them sore throats, and dealing with the usual barrage of questions from people – few of whom have any real intention of buying one of their products – will have left most of them frustrated and exhausted.

It is the same with every company, and even the most experienced car salesman can have difficulty in sorting out the genuine customers from the time-wasters. What percentage of the people who visit the Rolls-Royce stand each year really have more than £100,000 to spend on a car?

The truth can probably be best summed up by the story of the salesman on the Rolls-Royce stand who was asked the way to the nearest gentleman's toilet by a milkman making the early morning deliveries to the show. The salesman thought for a minute, then insisted on showing him the way himself. He then took the milkman across to the bar for a drink.

The bemused milkman couldn't understand why his simple request had caused such a surprising reaction, and after his third glass of champagne he plucked up enough courage to ask why:

"Tell me, governor, what do you want to entertain me for?" he asked, as his glass was being filled yet again. "Here are you, selling motor cars worth hundreds of thousands of pounds, and here am I, an ordinary milkman, like my father and grandfather before me. There is no way that I will ever have enough money to buy a Rolls-Royce so what do you want to entertain me for?"

"The answer is quite simple," the salesman replied with a broad grin. "Your inquiry was the first really honest one I've had all week!"

NO SECRET ANY MORE

Most new models take a minimum of three years to produce from the drawingboard and clay model stages, through to the first cars coming off the production line. Keeping their details secret is a nightmare for any motor manufacturer, particularly after the new models have reached the stage when prototypes need to be tested, and that usually means taking them abroad. The moment news leaks out that a model is being replaced, even by a modified version, sales of the old model drop off quickly and price-cutting begins. Manufacturers naturally want to prevent that from happening, but this can sometimes prove impossible.

The Sunbeam Rapier, which went on to become such a brilliant rally car, remained a closely guarded secret until an amateur photographer, who was a member of the Silver City Airways staff at Lydd Airport in Kent, photographed the prototype when it was waiting to be taken on board one of Silver City's Bristol Freighters which was flying it to France for testing.

There was an understanding at Rootes that the backup cars accompanying any prototype being taken abroad should always be the product of another car company, to put people off the scent. The company's engineering department always bought our competitor's latest models, to see how they performed against their own, and so there were usually plenty of them available. On this occasion, however, they were all being used elsewhere and the test team had to use a Hillman Minx estate car as their backup vehicle. Fortunately for me, this turned out to be a stroke of luck when the pictures were taken.

When the test team arrived at the airport with the Sunbeam Rapier prototype and the Hillman Minx estate car, they had to leave the keys of both vehicles for the Silver City staff to load them onto the aircraft. While our engineers' passports and papers were being checked inside the terminal building, however, unknown to them Silver City's amateur photographer was photographing the Sunbeam Rapier prototype from all angles. That evening he sent copies of the photographs to every national newspaper in Fleet Street.

Fortunately, the Hillman Minx estate car misled him and the captions on the photographs referred to the mysterious prototype as being a new Hillman. The new Rapier was very different in shape and size from any other Sunbeam, being smaller and closer in size to the Minx, and that was the reason why the following day I had calls from every daily and evening newspaper in London, telling me that the cat was out of the bag and they now had photographs of our new Hillman which they planned to publish. I was able to assure them that they certainly did not have photographs of any new Hillman prototype and promised that if a new Hillman was announced within the next 12 months, I would make sure that they all had one free of charge to give as a prize to their readers.

My assurance worked and none of the photographs were used, but when the new Sunbeam Rapier was announced and the papers realized that they had been sitting on photographs of it for nearly six months, some of the editors were understandably rather annoyed. They had to agree, however, that I had been entirely truthful, and that if they had published photographs of the new Sunbeam Rapier six months before it was due to be announced, the cost to Rootes in lost sales of other Sunbeam models could have run into millions of pounds; it was my job to prevent that from happening.

We weren't as fortunate, however, with the fuel injection version of the Rapier a few years later. Two of our engineers spent several weeks on the Continent testing the new 'hush hush' equipment, but as everything was safely hidden beneath the bonnet of a standard-looking Sunbeam Rapier, there didn't seem a need for any particular precautions.

They stayed for a night at a small hotel in Holland which didn't have a garage, thinking that the prototype would be safe if they parked it under cover at a local garage a few hundred yards away.

They were discussing the car's performance that day while they were having a drink in the hotel bar before dinner, but unfortunately their conversation was overheard by the garage proprietor, who was also having dinner in the hotel.

After they had gone to bed, he succeeded in opening up the test car and wiring the ignition. We found out later that he had spent the rest of the night driving it on a nearby fast stretch of road, taking performance figures and then photographing all the fuel injection equipment and the engine compartment, before returning the car to the garage and winding the mileometer back to the previous mileage so that the Rootes engineers wouldn't know that anything had happened to it while they had been asleep.

I didn't know anything about the garage proprietor's subterfuge until some weeks later, when all the car's performance figures, along with a double-page spread of pictures, appeared in a leading Dutch motoring journal. It was too late to do anything about it, and taking action against the garage proprietor would only have drawn more attention to the car and our new fuel injection system. It was one of those occasions when we had to grin and bear it and admit that we had been outwitted. Some you win, some you lose.

We chose an unfortunate day for the launch of another new Sunbeam. This time the motoring writers had been with us in France, test-driving the car in the Mediterranean sun, before attending the official press launch at Devonshire House. I had taken a group of them to the Wellington Club for lunch when there was an urgent telephone call for Basil Cardew of the *Daily Express*. He returned a few minutes later with the news that most of the Manchester United football team, Matt Busby's famous babes, had been killed in a tragic air crash at Munich. As we expected, all the reports and special features on the new car were taken out of the following day's papers to make way for reports on the crash and articles on Manchester United. What we didn't expect, however, was the decision of all the editors to publish the special features on the Sunbeam the following day, 24 hours after the launch. The business about the Sunbeam Rapier prototype photographs had obviously been forgotten and their decision meant a great deal to the success of the launch.

SPOT THE ALPINE

My colleagues and I were sometimes rather sceptical about what we considered to be security lapses by Rootes' engineers when they took prototypes abroad, but I had a much better understanding of the problems they faced after my wife and I had taken the prototype of the Sunbeam Alpine sportscar with us on holiday to *Le Lavendou*, in the South of France. The designers were rightly proud of their new car and thought that I would be as enthusiastic as they were if I had a proper opportunity to find out how the Alpine performed before the new sportscar went into production. The prototype didn't have any distinguishing badges and so we didn't expect that it would be noticed among all the other sportscars in the South of France. How wrong I was.

We had only reached as far as Rouen when the car was spotted for the first time. It was a hot day, the hood was down and we were held up at the lights in the town centre. I noticed that a group of young men, who had been taking more than a casual interest in the car, were crossing the road to get a better look. One of them, who had a broad Birmingham accent, turned to his friends and said: "What did I tell you? It is the new Sunbeam Alpine. That will give the French something to think about won't it?" Fortunately, the lights changed and I was able to accelerate away before he could ask me any awkward questions.

I'd no idea how he knew about the Alpine, but I began to relax again as we reached the open road and the speedometer needle approached the magic 100mph (161km/h). Suddenly there was a loud bang as one of the rear tyres blew out. By the time I had slowed down enough to pull in to a garage a few hundred yards further down the road, the tyre was ruined. We therefore left the car for a new tyre to be fitted while we went for a drink at a cafe and bar across the road.

We were joined there a few minutes later by the garage proprietor who seemed anxious to find out more about the car. I told him, quite correctly, that it was not a production model and that there were many British sportscars which could be made from kits. That answer didn't seem to satisfy him and he continued asking questions. I thought we had better be on our way as soon as possible and turned down his offer to check the oil.

When we were leaving and he handed me his business card, I realized why he had asked so many questions and been so keen to look under the bonnet. Below his name were the words 'Correspondent pour *L'Auto Journal*', the famous French motoring magazine which specialized in publishing details of new models well ahead of their announcement dates. Had he opened the bonnet to check the oil he would have seen the word 'Sunbeam' written in large letters across the engine cover.

I breathed a sigh of relief when we eventually reached *Le Lavendou* and parked the car by the harbour while I went to buy a newspaper. When I returned a few minutes later my wife was deep in conversation with a tall, dark-haired Frenchman. He opened the car door as I approached and said:

"You probably don't remember me, Mr Bullock, but I am a waiter at the Leofric Hotel in Coventry and when I saw you and your wife pull up in the new Sunbeam Alpine, I felt I must come and speak to you."

He explained that he lived near the Rootes factory in Coventry where the prototype Alpines had been made and had seen them going out on test. He was in *Le Lavendou* visiting his family.

Rather than taking any further chances of the Alpine being recognized while we were there, I parked it in a lockup garage and hired a Renault. Not so much fun to drive, but far less worrying to be seen with on holiday.

PUSH-PULL PARKING

Parking problems are not new, particularly in major towns and cities, but short of banning cars altogether, nobody has come up with an adequate answer. More cars could be parked in the streets if there was less space between them and motorists didn't need that extra bit of room in which to manoeuvre.

An American, Villor P Williams, thought he had the answer in 1927 when he invented his Parkmobile attachment, which slid beneath the car and lifted it clear of the ground on four jacking legs. The driver could then push the car sideways between two parked vehicles and pull it out into the main stream of the traffic when he wanted to drive off again. All very good in theory, but not very good in practice, particularly if the car was rather heavy or the road had a considerable camber and may be on a steep hill.

Parking could then be a very unpredictable manoeuvre and a parked car could end up on the pavement, or some distance away, even in another street, by the time the owner returned.

GOOD OLD UNCLE CHARLIE

Salesmen on the Rolls-Royce stand at motor show time had to be on their guard when Uncle Charlie was around, as I found out when Peter Collins and I took him on his annual pilgrimage "to buy his new Roller" as he put it. There was no doubting Peter Collins' courage at the wheel of a Grand Prix racing car, but his nerve seemed to fail him when he had to cope with a visit from Uncle Charlie and he was quickly on the telephone to me for support.

When I pleaded a prior engagement, he insisted I should help him out as payment for past favours. There was nothing I could do but give in. Uncle Charlie had his usual suite at the Savoy Hotel and Peter arranged that we would meet him in the cocktail lounge, take him to lunch and then on to the motor show, using the special guest tickets I had managed to acquire.

It all seemed quite straightforward. Uncle Charlie was a multi-millionaire friend of Peter's father, who came to London from South Africa each year for the express purpose of visiting the motor show, buying a new Rolls-Royce and savouring the delights of English draught beer, the thing he missed most since going to live in South Africa. He'd made his millions supplying steel to the Austin Motor Company when it was in short supply and while still in his early forties had retired and gone to live in the sun. The annual visit to London was a ritual he'd been following for close on 20 years.

Peter and I arrived at the Savoy Hotel in good time, chose a table in the corner of the cocktail lounge and had just settled down with a couple of gin and tonics when a large barrel-chested man walked in, grabbed Peter in a bear hug and then shook me by the hand with a grip that left my fingers numb. Uncle Charlie had obviously arrived.

"Ullo, Peter my boy," he said, with obvious pleasure, "I'd 'ave invited you up to 'ave a drink in the suite, but me lady friend isn't quite wot you would call decent, if you know what I mean."

He gave a knowing wink and his bronzed face broke into a broad grin as he stretched out in a chair and signalled to the waiter. Seeing our half-empty glasses he told him:

"We'll want the same again and I'll have a pint of best bitter, but make sure the gins are large ones, none of your short measures."

For some reason Uncle Charlie's appearance was not what I had expected it to be for a multi-millionaire. He was wearing an expensive suit, but the top button of his silk shirt was undone to reveal a rather hairy chest and his tie was hanging loosely, as though he had started to do it up and then changed his mind.

The rather young waiter was obviously also unimpressed by Uncle Charlie's appearance, or his request for a pint of best bitter, and said in a rather derogatory manner, "I'm sorry, but we don't serve draught beer in here. This is the cocktail lounge. Perhaps you would prefer to move to the bar."

Uncle Charlie gave a roar and his voice, despite its hoarseness, carried across the room to the head waiter, who was serving some drinks at a table in the corner. He rushed across as his young colleague was being told in no uncertain manner that if he didn't produce a pint of beer sharpish and if he gave Uncle Charlie any more of his lip, he'd be for it.

The head waiter was full of apologies, explaining that he hadn't seen Uncle Charlie arrive, but of course he could have his usual pint of bitter. It was just that the young waiter was new and didn't know the ropes.

"All I want", said Uncle Charlie with a grunt, "is a pint of bitter and for this young man to go away and bring me one, without any more of his lip and lecturing me on where I can and can't have a drink."

The head waiter brought our gin and tonics while his young assistant disappeared in the direction of the bar, returning a few minutes later with a pint of bitter in a silver tankard. Uncle Charlie picked it up, looked closely at it and asked,

"Do you think you could you get a large whisky in this?"

It was a very old joke, but whatever he said he was in for a hiding to nothing.

"I'm sure I could" the assistant replied, with as much enthusiasm as a lamb about to be slaughtered.

"In that case", said Uncle Charlie, grinning happily, "you can take it away and fill it up with beer. I don't approve of short measures, particularly when I am paying Savoy prices."

It was obvious that having got his pint of bitter – and the better of the young waiter – Uncle Charlie was beginning to enjoy himself. By the time lunch was over he was in a mellow mood and seemed all ready to go and choose his new car.

There were only a few people on the Rolls-Royce stand when we arrived, but none of the salesmen showed any interest in Uncle Charlie and busied themselves elsewhere whenever he tried to catch their eye. He went round each model in turn, but found all the doors locked.

"Here young man," he said, catching hold of a less nimble salesman by the arm. "What's wrong with these doors? I can't open any of them."

The salesman gave Uncle Charlie a rather supercilious smile. "Precisely sir" he said, attempting to move away. "They are locked to prevent you from opening them and sitting in any of the cars."

Uncle Charlie seemed as though he was about to explode:

"How can I decide whether I want to buy a new Rolls if I can't sit in it? Now are you going to open up the doors like a good lad?"

The salesman tried to break loose, but Uncle Charlie tightened his grip. The salesman shook his head:

"I'm afraid that is quite impossible" he said. "It's company policy that the doors must remain locked".

The multi-millionaire looked as though a blood vessel was about to burst when there was a shout from the other side of the stand.

"There you are Uncle Charlie, I've been looking everywhere for you."

Jack Barclay, the wealthy West End Rolls-Royce dealer, beamed as he rushed across, arms outstreched, and hugged Uncle Charlie.

"Glad to see you have been taking a look at our new models. What do you think of them?"

Jack Barclay took Uncle Charlie by the arm and led him across to the most expensive model.

"Not much" Uncle Charlie replied, glaring at the embarrassed salesmen. "The doors won't open and there must be something wrong with the upholstery because they don't want anyone to sit in them. I think I might be better off keeping the one I have."

For a moment I almost felt sorry for the salesman as Jack Barclay, hardly able to contain his anger, told him not to be such an idiot, adding "You've offended one of our most important customers. Surely you can distinguish between a time-waster and someone who has flown halfway round the world in order to buy a new Rolls!"

Jack Barclay had a point. Customers who did that each year were few and far between and deserved humouring, even cantankerous old roughnecks like Uncle Charlie.

A HEALTH HAZARD IN ITALY

Motor shows can easily become a health hazard for those who have to attend the never-ending list of official cocktail parties, lunches, dinners and new product launches. My last visit to the Turin show involved an unexpected health hazard. I only found out about it later, but it could have been more threatening to my wellbeing than too many gin and tonics, or too much good food and wine.

At the time I was about to leave Chrysler and set up a new public relations company. My friend Sir Barrie Heath invited me to fly with him to Turin in his company plane and be his guest for a week, for old times' sake. As I had to be in Turin and the motor show was also going to be the last function Barrie attended as President of the Society of Motor Manufacturers and Traders, there seemed a double reason for us to celebrate. Although there were a number of official functions we would have to attend, there should have been plenty of time left for us to enjoy ourselves.

The Italian papers were full of reports of kidnappings, shootings and threats to leading Italian industrialists. There were also suggestions that the terrorists might chose motor show time to target one of the international company heads. If so, the British President of the SMMT would be an obvious choice.

This didn't seem to worry Barrie and we didn't give it much thought when we took off from Luton Airport in his company jet, but on arrival in Turin he was annoyed to find that the SMMT had take the precaution of hiring a couple of minders, who insisted on being with him from morning to night. Barrie was a much-decorated wartime fighter pilot and didn't approve of so much fuss. Even though they were staying in the same hotel, he did manage to get away from them occasionally to have some fun with our motor industry friends by pretending to go off to bed and then slip by them when they retired to the bar.

During the day I enjoyed riding around in his official car, with its police escort. It saved taxi fares and ensured that there weren't any parking problems, because Barrie always received VIP treatment when we arrived at the show. I didn't give any thought to the occasions when he insisted that I should take his official car, saying that he was making a last-minute alteration to a speech he was giving, and I didn't think it strange when he said he would follow on later, rather than keep the official car parked outside the hotel.

On the flight home he opened a bottle of champagne and said:

"Well that's over and we've both escaped the clutches of the terrorists."

"What do you mean we've both escaped their clutches? You're the one they'd have been after, not me. I was never in any kind of danger," I replied as he filled my glass.

"You were while you were driving around in my official car," he chuckled. "There were several warnings from the Italian police during the show about a possible kidnap attempt. I knew it was all a lot of nonsense, but swapping cars kept them happy and I didn't want to worry you. The police thought that if you were kidnapped, the terrorists would be more likely to let you go when they realized their mistake."

"What if they didn't?" I asked.

"Then I would have arranged the ransom. After all, what are friends for? I'd have done the same for you!"

What indeed?

A GOLD-PLATED FLOP AND A SPORTING SENSATION

Apart from providing a shop window for the car companies to show off their latest products, international motor shows focus media attention on the motor industry over a quite lengthy period. When it comes to show time, publicity is the name of the game and there is nothing like a good gimmick to create media interest in some of the older models – the cars, that is, not the two-legged variety!

It is usually the sportscars and more popular family saloons which get the gimmick treatment and have the partly-clad girls draped across their bonnets on press day and television personalities available on the stand to pose with them. They can add that little extra interest to a news photograph and perhaps provide a few lines of copy for the gossip columnists.

Publicizing new models is not difficult. It is getting some of the older ones noticed among the glittering galaxy of new cars on show that calls for something out of the ordinary. It is even more difficult if the model is a rather staid luxury saloon, whose most noticeable feature is the price.

For more than 50 years, until Nora Docker arrived on the scene, the Daimler Company produced a range of expensive luxury saloons which appealed to members of the royal family, government ministers and company chairmen, but which didn't attract much motor show coverage, because they were looked upon as being rather boring by the majority of news editors. Nora certainly changed that for Daimler. A former Birmingham barmaid, millionaires were attracted to her like flies to a honey pot and those who proposed marriage included Sir Bernard Docker, the Daimler Chairman and a leading Midlands industrialist.

The Daimler Company was proud of its royal connections, which dated back to 1898 when the Prince of Wales, who later became King Edward VII, had his first ride in a Daimler. He became the first royal car owner in June 1900, after the outstanding success Daimlers had in the first Thousand Miles Trial that year. When King George later purchased a fleet of Daimlers, the company became quite carried away and in 1926 built him a gigantic model, with a 7.1-litre 12-cylinder engine, which they hoped would be the quietest and most vibration-free car ever built. It was, but proved so expensive to run that even the king couldn't afford it. From then on they concentrated on outstanding design and engineering perfection.

During the company's Jubilee celebrations at London's Savoy Hotel in 1946, Lord Brabazon described the Daimler car as "having become a national institution", but all that changed when Nora Docker began making her presence felt in the Daimler boardroom. She was responsible for the outrageously finished 'Docker Daimlers' and insisted on using the comedian Norman Wisdom to publicize them. Unfortunately, his portrayal of a simple, downtrodden little man, in a schoolboy cap and suit several sizes too small, was hardly the right image for an expensive luxury car intended for royalty and top company executives.

The gold-plated model she had made for the Earls Court motor show also went down like a lead balloon. Apart from appearing ostentatious, which Daimler owners didn't like, the gold plate lacked the sparkle of chrome and looked more like dirty brass. I went to see it before the show opened and overheard two cockney cleaners discussing what was intended to be Lady Docker's gold star attraction.

"Ere," said one, "what do you think of that, then? A posh motor like that 'aving brass bumpers and door handles. You'd think they could have afforded to 'ave some chrome."

I couldn't resist telling them that what they thought was brass was really gold. They gave me a long hard look and then burst out laughing.

"He must think we're barmy" one remarked, as they disappeared with their buckets and brooms. The public thought that the 'Docker Daimlers' were also barmy, and unfortunately so did many of the company's usual customers. Not long afterwards Daimler was in serious trouble. The company lost its royal patronage and Sir Bernard was asked to resign his chairmanship amid serious allegations of extravagance and mismanagement. The Dockers' image was further blighted when Prince Rainier banned them and their yacht from Monte Carlo. Daimler never recovered from Nora's interference in its affairs and had to be saved by Jaguar in 1960. Gimmicks are all right if they fit in with a car's successful image. When they don't, they can do more harm than good.

The Daimler Company's entry into the sportscar field was also a source of considerable embarrassment when the early models of the hyped-up Daimler Dart had serious body troubles and leaked like a sieve. It was particularly unfortunate that it was raining hard when the *Autocar* team arrived to put it through its paces and publish their early impressions on the company's new sportscar.

After a very wet drive, they arrived back at the factory with soaking wet trousers, as the Dart's seats had gradually become sodden with rain. The *Autocar*'s test drivers were hurriedly taken to the boardroom and given warming drinks, while their trousers were taken away and dried before they drove back to London. Fortunately, the body problems were overcome and the model became a reasonable success.

A SPORTING SENSATION

It is usually the sportscars from the large, well established companies which become the stars of any international motor show, but that wasn't the case in 1952. The Healey 100 came from a small company, and certainly didn't need any gimmicks to attract media attention. The amazing reception it received when it made a last-minute appearance at that year's Earls Court motor show, even though it was only partly finished, had to be seen to be believed.

The car was the brainchild of Donald Healey, a chirpy, First World War fighter pilot from Cornwall, who had made his name in international rallies and trials, some of which he did with Ian Fleming, of *James Bond* fame, as navigator. He became the first Englishman to win the Monte Carlo Rally outright when he drove a 4½-litre Invicta to victory with Humphrey Symonds and Lewis Pearce in 1931, despite hitting a tree and damaging the braking system.

Donald began designing cars after the war on the kitchen table at his house with the help of Ben Bowden and 'Sammy' Sampietro, when all three were working for the Rootes brothers in Coventry. Sampietro was an Italian who had been released from internment during the war to work for Rootes because of his valuable engineering skills. All three continued to work for the Rootes brothers while they concentrated on designing their new sportscar. They had help from the WAAFs at a local RAF station in tracing all the drawings, and a friend of Donald's, who owned a works in Warwick making cement mixers, let them use a spare shed he had there, along with some cement mixer machine tools, so that they could build the chassis. The Riley company gave them an engine and offered to build the first body, and as soon as the prototype was ready Donald made further use of his RAF friends by persuading the Commanding Officer at RAF Honiley, near Warwick, to let them use the airfield for testing its performance. The main runway was just long enough for the car to reach 100mph, but every test run ended in a furious dice as they had to brake hard in order to turn onto the perimeter track before going through the hedge at the end.

The Donald Healey Motor Company came into existence in 1946 with a capital of £50,000. The racing and rally experience the company gained with their early models led to work starting in 1951 on a new sportscar aimed mainly at the American market, and making use of the engine from the Austin A90 Atlantic, which had never been a popular car despite holding various production car records. Just before the opening of the Earls Court motor show in 1952, the prototype Healey 100 was taken to Belgium where it reached 110mph on the Jabbeke Highway. Donald Healey still wasn't satisfied with the look of the radiator grille and to stop any head-on photographs from being taken during the show, the car was pushed up against a concrete pillar on the stand so that only three-quarter views were possible. This was a stroke of luck, because the pillar protected the car from the thousands of people who swarmed round it every day during the show.

The Healey 100 was a sensation from the moment the doors opened and one of the first to visit the stand was Sir Leonard Lord, the Austin Motor Company chief, and he brought along Lord Nuffield and George Harriman. Sir Leonard did a deal with Donald-Healey in his hotel that evening for the name to be changed to the Austin-Healey 100 and for the car to be built at Longbridge. Overnight the pretty little winged Healey 100 badge was redesigned to include the Austin name and Donald Healey's new model proved to be one of the most successful sportscars produced since the war. It also helped restore the fortunes of the Austin company in America.

A gold-plated Austin-Healey, with an ivory steering wheel and mink upholstery, was built for a later motor show. Ken Gregory, who had been Stirling Moss' racing manager until Donald Healey took him on as his first PRO, thought up the idea and the gold-plated Austin-Healey was far more successful than Lady Docker's gold-plated Daimler. It certainly appealed to one American sportscar enthusiast, who bought the show model and had it shipped to the United States.

It is not clear whether the mink upholstery was such a great success, though. Lorna Snow, the glamorous international rally driver, usually chose leopard skin upholstery for her personalized white Jaguar. "Mink is too hot to sit on and not to be recommended for a car," she explained when I asked why she didn't go for mink instead of leopard. That must come as a relief to many husbands!

Motor manufacturers are always looking for ways of attracting photographers to their stands on motor show press days in the hope of

getting those extra column-inches. The outfits worn by the models who draped themselves over the bonnets of each new design seemed to get skimpier each year, until the inevitable happened and topless and even nude models appeared.

Hundreds of photographs were taken of them and the cars they were draped over, but to my knowledge none were ever published. It was before the days of 'Page Three' girls and newspapers were still not prepared to publish nude photographs for fear of upsetting many of their readers.

The photographers had a field day, however, and newspaper darkrooms were covered in the new nude model photographs. While the girls were posing, cameras appeared as if by magic and there were cries of "Bend over a little bit more", and "Can you take a deep breath and lean further across the bonnet?"

The models didn't realize that very often the photographers had already used up all their film and their cameras were empty. They were simply getting the girls to pose for the benefit of their newspaper colleagues and the large crowd of onlookers.

A RATTLING GOOD HUSKY

An unsolved noise in any car can be infuriating, but a persistent rattle in a brand-new model, particularly one which had been bought by a motoring magazine to test its quality and reliability, was obviously a problem which needed solving without delay. The Hillman Husky purchased by the *Autocar* magazine developed not only a continuous body rattle, but also a rather pungent smell in the rear passenger compartment which became steadily worse. It soon became known on the magazine as 'a real stinker' which nobody wanted to drive; anyone who did had to go along with the windows open.

The dealer who supplied the car had to admit defeat and the same thing happened when it was sent to the main Rootes Service Centre at Ladbroke Hall, in North London. Rootes offered to replace it, but the *Autocar* understandably still wanted to know what made their new Husky rattle so badly and generate such an unpleasant smell.

The only solution I could think of was to send the smelly Husky back to the Rootes factory in Coventry, where it had been built, then have it stripped down a piece at a time until the body engineers discovered the real cause of the problem. The mystery was quickly solved as soon as the outer body panels were removed. A glass milk bottle was resting on one of the crossmembers and had obviously been held there by the outer metal panels of the body and the interior trim. It was still partly full of milk, which had gone off and solidified and was producing an offensive smell similar to that of a leaking gasometer.

The mystery of how it got there was also solved when the foreman in the paint shop remembered an employee who had been very fond of milk and used to take a bottle with him into the spray booth. He must have put the partly drunk bottle down for a moment onto one of the Husky's crossmembers. Before he could remove it, the conveyor took the car and the bottle on to the trim section. Somehow it escaped notice during the trimming process and the employee didn't report it missing.

Although it proved to be a very expensive and well-travelled bottle of milk, it did make an amusing story for the magazine. After the Husky had been returned to the *Autocar*, without its offending milk bottle, it proved to be a 'rattling good buy' and didn't give any further trouble during the two years it was in constant use there.

A ROLLS-ROYCE MUCK-SPREADER

Owning a Rolls-Royce remains a cherished dream for most people, but there have been occasions when owners have treated 'The Best Car in the World' with what could only be described as disdain bordering on contempt. Take the case of the Lincolnshire farmer I came across soon after the war, who had cut the roof off his Rolls-Royce 40/50 saloon and was using the car for muck-spreading. His actions didn't seem to cause much surprise at the time because the average cost of a prewar 40/50 Rolls-Royce saloon was about £50 and people weren't queueing up to buy them.

The model's large, thirsty engine was enough to put most people off owning one in petrol-starved Britain, and the Lincolnshire farmer was probably running his on some other concoction like TVO anyway. Farmers were also allowed the dreaded red petrol, banned for ordinary motorists, who were fined heavily if the police found traces of it in their petrol tanks.

Imagine what that farmer's muck-spreading vehicle would be worth now:

certainly many times the cost of a brand-new muck-spreader! During the First World War cars were frequently stored away in barns, covered with a dust sheet and then left because their owners could no longer afford to run them, or had gone away to war. Years later many of them were still gathering dust and had become forgotten, because their original owners had been killed, died or moved away. Old cars were of little interest, except to a few wealthy enthusiasts who had the time and space needed to enjoy such a hobby.

During the Twenties a friend of my father's was fortunate to have both and collecting old cars became one of his main interests. While he was in Wales, the proprietor of the hotel where he was staying told him about an old car which a local farmer had found in his barn and had been trying to get rid of because he needed the space for storage.

He hurried to the farm the following morning and saw what was obviously a prewar car covered in dust and muck. It was clear that the hens had been roosting in it for some time and it had been pushed into the corner of a barn out of the way. The vehicle was surrounded by junk and old farm implements, which made it difficult to tell its age or make, but there seemed little doubt that it was an open tourer built sometime before the war.

The farmer had been prepared to pay to have it taken away and jumped at the offer of a £5 note. A trailer was sent for and when enough space had been made for the car to be wheeled into the open, there was no doubt that it was an early Rolls-Royce, which had probably been standing in the barn since the start of the First World War. After it had been taken away, cleaned and stripped down, the excited new owner realized that only a few parts were required to make it run again and he wrote to Rolls-Royce, quoting the car's chassis and engine number in the hope that they might still be able to help.

The result was hardly what he had expected. The following morning there was an urgent telephone call from the company to say that two engineers were on their way to look at the car. Even by Rolls-Royce standards, that seemed like incredible service for one of their owners whose car was not only several years old, but also in a poor state of repair.

The engineers spent the morning studying the car and checking it with documents they had brought with them. When they had finished they offered the bemused owner the option of £3,000 or a new Rolls-Royce in exchange for the delapidated car which he had rescued from the Welsh barn. They had verified it as one of the first 40/50 Silver Ghosts, of which the company had lost trace and wanted for their own museum.

Events have shown that he made the wrong choice and should have held on to the old car instead of swapping it for a new one, but he wasn't to know then that a car he'd rescued from a barn would one day be worth hundreds of thousands of pounds. How many people are there now who would turn down the offer of a new Rolls-Royce?

The stories are, of course, legion about 'The Best Car in the World', the title given to Rolls-Royce by Lord Northcliffe, after he had taken delivery of his first Rolls-Royce Silver Ghost. He was a friend of Claude Johnson, who had been the Hon. Charles Rolls' partner when he met Henry Royce. The company adopted his slogan and the majority of models have lived up to it for nearly 90 years.

Every effort has been made to retain the mystique and ensure that owners of a Rolls-Royce get a service second to none. The advertisement after the war, informing people that the noisiest aspect of their latest model was the ticking of the clock, was probably correct. Few car makers, if any, could make such a claim even in the Nineties.

Before the start of the Second World War, Rolls-Royce sent an engineer to America with some replacement parts and instructions to track down every owner of a particular model and check every car for a possible steering fault. The checks were to be done free of charge and the suspect parts changed, if possible, without the owner knowing. His task was only partly completed when war started and he had to call a halt, but as soon as the war ended he was told to finish the job he'd set out to do, which he did without any further interruption.

A rather less spectacular, but nevertheless impressive example of Rolls-Royce service was witnessed by a colleague of mine in the early Fifties, who had been sent the latest model to road-test. The starter motor had jammed while the car was parked outside his London flat and he and his wife were about to go out for dinner. He telephoned the Rolls-Royce PRO at home and shortly afterwards a large plain van arrived with two mechanics. They opened the back of the vehicle, winched the car inside and closed it up again.

It only took a matter of minutes for the fault to be rectified, the car to be backed out onto the road and for the van and mechanics to disappear into the night. It was obvious that Rolls-Royce didn't want anybody to see their mechanics working in the road on a new Rolls-Royce and knew how to deal efficiently with the situation when it arose.

There are, of course, those occasions when a Rolls-Royce breaks down and there is nothing the company can do, except hope that their reputation will not be tarnished too much. It happened when Rootes were hosting a dinner for some important motoring editors from Scandinavia. They were on a visit to Britain organized by the Society of Motor Manufacturers and Traders. We had arranged to send two of our latest Humber Super Snipes to the airport to take the editors and their luggage to their hotel and then bring them on to Quaglinos for the dinner, which had been arranged in a private room.

At the last minute I had a call from the SMMT to say that Rolls-Royce were very keen to collect our dinner guests from the airport, so that the motoring editors could ride in their latest model. I agreed, but started to get worried when they didn't arrive at the restaurant as planned and a telephone call revealed that they hadn't even arrived at their hotel.

When they did eventually arrive for dinner, more than an hour late, we learned that one of the cars taking them to their hotel had broken down on the way into London from the airport. To make matters worse, one of the overseas editors had carried out the running repairs needed get it going.

It made a good story for him, but not the one Rolls-Royce intended. My sympathies went out to them, even though it was their faulty car which had been responsible for messing up our dinner party. Although it was encouraging to know that even 'The Best Car in the World' broke down occasionally, for that to happen with important overseas motoring editors on board was the sort of bad luck I wouldn't have wished on any competitor, or at least not a British one!

A MINX AND THE *PAVE* KIDS

One record-breaking performance by a British car which can never be broken involved five well-known women rally drivers and an ordinary Hillman Minx. The year was 1959, and all over Europe there was a feeling that British cars were not made to last. We decided that the best way of answering that criticism would be for a family saloon like the Hillman Minx to cover 25,000km, virtually non-stop, over the worst cobbled *pave* in Europe.

The obvious place for the attempt was Belgium, a country which had just doubled its quota of British cars and still had a few hundred miles of famous Belgian *pave*, the cobblestone roads, that would test any car's ability to stay in one piece, particularly if it was driven over them at speed for any length of time.

After several weeks of searching we succeeded in finding a route in the Brussels area which was all *pave*, but doing so had proved much more difficult than we had expected because most of the *pave* had already been dug up and replaced as part of the country's major road-building programme. Sections of the *pave* which remained were also being torn up every day and we realized that our record-breaking attempt would have to be a fight against time, as well as a test of the car's ability to stay the course.

After studying Belgian military maps borrowed from the army, and weeks of driving round the Brussels area asking local residents if they knew where any sections of *pave* remained, a 112-mile test route was worked out in the shape of a giant loop to the north-east of the city. It started in the suburbs and then went through Vilvoorde, Michelen, Boom, Mortsel, Lier, Herenhort, Westmeerback, Aarschot,and Hacht. Some of the roads were little more than tracks and just wide enough for a car, passing through farmyards, over railway crossings and across swing-bridges.

Women rally drivers had been chosen to show that brute strength wasn't required. There was also the thought that a spot of glamour would provide better photographic opportunities. Sheila Van Damm, the former Women's European Rally Champion, whose father owned London's famous Windmill Theatre, was persuaded to come out of retirement to lead the team. The other four members were Nancy Mitchell, another former European Rally Champion; Mary Handley Page, of the famous aircraft family, who had taken over from Sheila as the captain of the Rootes women's rally team; Francoise Clarke and Pat 'Tish' Ozanne.

They all arrived in Brussels early in February, with Norman Garrad, the Rootes Competitions Manager, and his team of mechanics and timekeepers. Their first task was to study the route and meet the members of the Belgian Royal Automobile Club who were to act as official observers. Monsieur M H de Harlez, the director of the sporting section of the Club, was in no doubt that we were all crazy. He told Norman Garrad and his women drivers "having seen the route I will eat my hat if your car does more than 500 miles under those road conditions".

He had the support of the British Motor Industry's Research Association, who assured us that it was extremely unlikely that any car could stand up to a battering on the *pave* for more than 1,000 miles, a distance they estimated to be the equivalent under those conditions to the normal life of a family car. They were quite adamant that we would fail in our attempt because the Research Association's Vehicle Analysis reports included a 1,000-miles *pave* test, and many new cars even failed to cover that much shorter distance on *pave*. However, nobody there would go so far as to offer to eat their hats if we succeeded.

Despite these warnings, that February a grey Hillman Minx saloon was taken from the Rootes assembly lines at Ryton-on-Dunsmore, near Coventry, to a nearby disused airfield to be run in for 4,000 miles. After being serviced it was then driven to Brussels, ready for the start of the 25,000km *pave* test. However, as a result of MIRA's and Monsieur de Harlez's negative forecasts, we decided not to inform the media about our plans in case the predictions proved correct; we would then be left looking very foolish.

Norman Garrad organized the event in Grand Prix style, using lap charts, an official log book and highly trained pit crews. Nothing was left to chance, and when Sheila Van Damm set off on the first lap at 8.30am on Tuesday, February 10, she was accompanied by an official observer from the Belgian RAC and Francois Clarke, who had volunteered to navigate for the first 10 hours until all the drivers had managed to memorize the test route and would be able to drive solo. It was Pancake Day and a Mardi Gras holiday for the local residents, who were puzzled for a time to see the same car going past them at regular intervals with different drivers at the wheel, but after a while they started looking out for the Minx and waving as it went past.

The car was a standard Minx saloon, apart from the floor gearshift and bucket seats, which were optional extras, two Lucas 700 foglamps and a set of Dunlop Gold Seal tyres. The Dunlop Tyre Company also provided us with a set of its experimental steel-studied ice tyres, which proved invaluable when the weather conditions deteriorated and the drivers had to contend with black ice. Because of the buffeting the Minx was getting and the strain of having to drive at high speed over narrow stretches of *pave*, which sometimes also contained deep potholes hidden by mud, the drivers were changed at the end of every second lap. To have gone on any longer would have caused too much strain and might have proved dangerous.

The ice tyres had to be fitted at the end of only five laps, after the atrocious weather and road conditions had increased the circuit lap time from an average of two hours 48 minutes to nearly four hours. With the new ice tyres the car began lapping again at two hours 53 minutes, much to everyone's relief.

A few hours later, however, the weather worsened and Brussels experienced the worst fog the city had known for more than 30 years. Visibility was reduced to only a few yards and the official observers refused to continue with the test until conditions improved. The Minx was brought in, sealed, and kept under guard until the fog lifted slightly and the observers agreed to go on. Apart from the brief refuelling stops, that was the only time that the engine was switched off for the duration of the test.

On lap 36 Mary Handley Page reported that the fog was so bad that she had been forced to stay in third gear all the way round the course and at the end of lap 45 Nancy Mitchell wrote in the log book: "My observer was ill twice and I had to lose 14 minutes when I stopped to give him time to recover."

By lap 50 the visibility was again down to about four yards, but because of the delays caused by the sick observer, everyone, including the Belgian officials, agreed to press on until the fog lifted and the weather eventually improved.

On the fifth day there was a panic when Sheila Van Damm reported an unusual rattle in the back of the car. One of the mechanics traced the mysterious noise to a half-empty tin of boiled sweets which one of the observers had left in the car. It had slipped down from the rear seat and was rolling about the floor.

During the second week the team was reduced to four when Nancy Mitchell flew back to England after learning that her daughter's baby had arrived. The other members of the team cabled her: 'Congratulations to the fastest granny in the business' and signed it 'The *Pave* Kids'. Nancy returned to Brussels after two days and with all five drivers back in action and the car running like clockwork, it began to look as though the experts who forecast disaster were going to be proved wrong. It was also noticeable that Monsieur de Harlez had started leaving his hat at home.

The Belgian papers were writing daily reports about the Minx, which they christened '*La Petite Folle*', the little mad girl, but we still had another very worrying problem which could have put paid to our chances of success. The Brussels rebuilding programme was going ahead at such a speed that two of the large buildings the drivers had been using as landmarks suddenly disappeared. Even more worrying was the speed with which the last of the *pave* was being torn up and replaced by tarmac roads; it really was touch and go as to whether the route would remain intact until the test had been completed. Our luck held, however, and with only a few thousand kilometres remaining before the 25,000km target was reached we felt the time had come to tell the press what we were doing.

We flew a party of about 40 British motoring journalists to Brussels on March 2, in time for them to witness the final laps and be taken round the circuit in one of the recce cars. When Sheila eventually crossed the finishing line, after completing the final lap to the cheers of the crowd that had gathered at various parts of the route, '*La Petite Folle*' had covered the 25,000km (15,534 miles) in 375 hours at an average speed of 41mph. The only parts replaced during the run had been a set of shock absorbers, which were changed during one of the refuelling stops, two speedometer cables and the windscreen wiper blades.

We were certainly relieved that everything had gone according to plan and the pessimists had been proved wrong. Monsieur de Harlez was there, still wisely without his hat, but his honour was salvaged when the *pave* kids had one made of marzipan. After the journalists had written their stories for the following morning's papers, we all went off for a celebratory dinner, while the exhausted drivers caught up on their lost sleep.

It was too late to fly back to England that night, but seats were booked on the first available flight out in the morning. However, nobody seemed to want to go to bed and so after dinner we decided to have a party at the *Moulin Rouge* night club. The Belgian papers had been full of the exploits of the five British girls and their Hillman Minx, and although it was approaching closing time at the club, the manager seemed happy to keep it open all night when he heard why we were celebrating. He even provided some free champagne. Although the band was already packing up, the two guitarists agreed to stay, and with Gregor Grant, the editor of *Autosport*, taking turns with me on the piano, we kept the celebrations going until five in the morning, after which everybody, including the manager and his staff, retired to a nearby cafe for bacon and eggs. It was certainly a night to remember and a fitting climax to a motoring achievement which can never be repeated. We just had time to collect our cases from the hotel and catch our plane to London.

The victorious Minx was shipped back to England and sent to the Motor Industry Research Association's testing ground near Nuneaton to be driven

to destruction. The Association's staff and our own engineers were keen to discover the full effects that the pounding on the *pave* had inflicted on a normal family saloon, and the information was passed on to our design team for use with later models. When all the tests had been completed, we made sure that the Minx was then scrapped beyond repair to prevent any chance of it being sold to a member of the public, who might have thought that they had purchased a bargain, a one-owner Minx with only 20,000 miles on the clock!

METRONOME PROBLEMS

As Chairman of the British Government's Dollar Export Council, Sir William Rootes, who was later made a Baron for his export achievements, was continually trying to persuade car companies to export more of their products to the dollar markets. The Rootes public relations team was kept at full stretch writing the speeches he had to make each week at business lunches and dinners.

Many of them were written by John Wilcox, who tried to enliven them with amusing anecdotes and stories, but whenever he did so he was faced with one serious problem: Billy Rootes was a brilliant entrepreneur, a super salesman, an exceptional businessman and an inspiring leader, but he had a very limited sense of humour, particularly when buying and selling was involved.

When John Wilcox was asked to write a speech about the need for companies to have patience when tackling the American market and to remember there were highs and lows during every overseas sales campaign, he likened the situation to a metronome, swinging from one extreme to the other, adding: "...and in case you don't know what a metronome is, it's a dwarf on the Paris underground."

Billy Rootes read the speech through carefully until he came across the reference to the metronome, and asked his brother, who was in the next office, to join him. As soon as Sir Reginald entered the room Billy Rootes said: "Reggie, what's a metronome?"

Sir Reginald looked rather surprised, but explained that it is an instrument people placed on a piano to keep time for a particular piece of music."

"I thought it was," Billy replied, "but this fool Wilcox thinks it's a dwarf on the Paris underground!"

I made a similar mistake when I was writing another dollar exports speech and suggested that some of the smaller British motor manufacturers could be as successful as David had been against Goliath, if they tackled the giant American export market the right way. All they needed was sufficient courage, the right ammunition and knowledge of the right areas of the market to target.

It was quite obvious that Billy didn't know who David and Goliath were, but I explained that they were characters from the Bible and he eventually agreed to leave them in his speech as an interesting synonym.

I was present when he made the speech, which went over very well until he reached the reference to David and Goliath. Unfortunately he referred to Goliath slaying David, instead of the other way round, and there was a rather baffled silence on the part of the audience.

As soon as he had finished and before waiting for the applause to die down, Billy made a bee-line for me, fuming:

"I told you, John, we shouldn't have said anything about David and Goliath. Doing so was a great mistake. They don't like religion in the motor industry."

I didn't quote from the Bible again in any of his speeches.

THE CRAIGEVAR EXPRESS

Although steam cars have had their day and Singer was probably the last major company to consider going into production with one when they built a steam-powered prototype in 1954, there was a period when they were the most popular cars on sale.

Some 80 different makes of steam car were sold between 1895 and 1930 and in 1906 a Stanley Steamer reached a remarkable 127mph on the Florida Sands, a speed beyond any petrol model at the time. They did have disadvantages, though.

For example, it took 20 minutes to get up steam from cold and if the driver accelerated too quickly the main fire was liable to blow out, which meant that pressurized paraffin would be sprayed all over the burners. If the main fire could be relighted quickly there was usually a loud plop and all was well, but it was necessary to stand well clear of the flash; many men who crowded too near had their moustaches and beards singed. In those days, motoring could be dangerous even before drivers and their passengers reached the open road.

The Stanley Steamer and the White Steam Car both had terrific acceleration and were dead quiet, but that certainly wasn't true of the Craigevar Express, built in Scotland in 1895 by Andrew Lawson, the 'Postie' at Alford, in Aberdeenshire, a year before the first Daimler car was made in Coventry and Britain's motor industry began. 'Postie' Lawson had a long beard, sideburns and was a fine figure of a man. Despite being rather grumpy, he was known to be very popular with many of the ladies in Alford and the surrounding villages, as well as with the children, who enjoyed playing on the merry-go-round he had built for use at village fetes. He was also a man of considerable ingenuity and foresight and constructed a water wheel alongside the burn at the bottom of his garden, to provide sufficient power for his cottage and workshop.

After his death, his steam car was rescued from a rubbish tip by Lord Sempill, the owner of Craigevar Castle, a keen motorist, aviator and a close friend of Maurice Smith, by then the Editorial Director of Illife Press. Maurice Smith had been a much-decorated pilot in the war, and during the late Forties and early Fifties, had the good fortune to be editor of both *Flight* and *Autocar* magazines during one of the most interesting periods in the development of aviation and motoring. As editor of *Flight* he had his own company plane, and one of his perks as editor of *Autocar*, then the most influential motoring magazine in Britain, was a new Aston Martin car each year.

I first saw 'Postie' Lawson's remarkable steam car soon after Lord Sempill's own death when his widow sold it to Maurice Smith, because she knew that he was a veteran car enthusiast and had already rebuilt a number of old cars. I agreed to go with him to Scotland to bring the Craigevar Express back to Surrey. We decided to use a Singer estate car from the Rootes press demonstration fleet because it was the only model available with a tow bar attachment, and we also managed to borrow quite a sizeable trailer, which we thought would be up to the steam car's weight.

We arrived at Craigevar Castle about mid-afternoon on the Saturday, but it was nearly dusk by the time we had finished having tea with Lady Sempill, loaded the steam car onto the trailer and covered it with a large tarpaulin. Our plan was to drive part of the way and stop overnight at a hotel somewhere near the border, but before setting off we stopped for a beer at the local pub and ordered some sandwiches so that we wouldn't need to stop for dinner.

Our sandwiches had just arrived when a number of local youths came into the pub and wanted to know what was under the tarpaulin on the trailer. With its large boiler and tall chimney it was obviously a steam car and we saw no point in denying the fact:

"That's not the Craigevar Express you have there?" asked one accusingly.

It seemed more like a threat than a question and the rather large Scotsman who wanted to know looked as though his favourite pastime was probably tossing the caber. It soon became apparent that he didn't approve of a couple of Sassenachs taking the famous steam car out of Scotland, even though it now belonged to one of them. There was a general murmur of approval when he went on:

"If it is and you have any idea of taking it out of Scotland, forget it. The Craigevar Express is not leaving here and that's a fact."

As all his friends seemed to hold the same view, Maurice and I realized that a situation was developing which could easily end in a fight, which we probably would lose as we were heavily outnumbered. If we were to make it back to England with the car that night we obviously had to make a move rather rapidly and it was a time for some quick thinking. We paid for another couple of beers and asked the landlord in a loud voice "the way to the gentlemen's", but as soon as we were through the door we both made a run for it.

Fortunately, it was only when they heard the car start that the local lads realized what had happened and gave chase. By that time we had several hundred yards' start and with the road winding downhill there was little chance of them getting past. It was a rather hairy drive, however, with the trailer and the Craigevar Express tied to it swaying about behind our car, but we managed to stay ahead until the local lads became fed up and decided to return to their beers.

Although they had broken off the chase, there was still a possibility that they would follow us to the border later as there was really only one road we could take. Maurice and I didn't want to run the risk of them catching up with us if we stopped, so we kept going until we were over the border into England and could be sure that the danger had passed. Having got that far, however, we decided to continue non-stop to Maurice's house at Ashtead, where our wives were waiting for us. We took turns to drive, which enabled each of us to cat-nap, and when we were only a few miles from home we did stop long enough to freshen up and have breakfast. We felt that our wives, who were not expecting us until after lunch, wouldn't want two bleary-eyed, unshaven and hungry husbands arriving on the doorstep at seven o'clock on the Sunday morning.

After the Craigevar Express had been unloaded from the trailer and wheeled into the garage, I had a chance to take a closer look at 'Postie' Lawson's remarkable vehicle. Constructed mainly of wood, it looked rather like a coster's large wooden handcart, with quite a small wheel at the front and two larger ones at the rear. It had tiller steering and was powered by a large boiler with a long chimney situated at the front. There were various controls within reasonable reach of the driver, but Maurice always claimed that he needed three hands to control the vehicle properly: one for the throttle, one for the steering and another for the brake. The engine was even older than the Craigevar itself, and had been used previously in a sawmill. Several bits required replacing, the boiler needed relining and parts of the ash frame also had to be renewed.

I was glad that we had succeeded in saving such a historic car, and after nearly a year's careful reconstruction, Maurice had it again in pristine condition and ready to be seen by other steam and veteran car enthusiasts. The Craigevar Express appeared frequently at steam rallies throughout the country, always attracting large crowds, and was the oldest coal-powered steam car to take part in the famous London-to-Brighton Emancipation Run. It failed to finish on the first occasion, but on the second time it reached Brighton within the time limit and with just four minutes to spare. Although the car's top speed was higher than the 16-18mph reached during the run, it would probably have gone out of control if full power had been used.

The locals who had tried to prevent the Craigevar Express from leaving Scotland finally had their wish in 1982 when, more than 25 years after our hasty departure with it, Maurice Smith arranged for the car to go to the Grampians Transport Museum Trust. 'Postie' Lawson's piece of motoring history is now back in Scotland for good, but Maurice's son Colin still visits the museum each year to drive the Craigevar Express during one of its many appearances at shows and other functions.

SOME FISHY FLIGHTS FROM ABERDEEN

Kipper enthusiasts will agree that few can match the taste and quality of a real Arbroath smoky, and most of the British press who went to Aberdeen for the launch of Chrysler's latest model didn't want to return home without a supply of them. To make sure that they had been freshly smoked, we sent for a fresh supply each morning and gave each guest a large packet of them as they left their hotel for the airport.

We had arranged with British Airways to reserve blocks of seats on the early morning flights to Birmingham and London, but had overlooked the effect that so many Arbroath smokies would have on the other passengers – particularly during the very hot weather. The idea was dropped following frantic calls from British Airways, pleading with us to find a less pungent Scottish delicacy for our guests. The kippers were even a problem after the aircraft had landed and arrangements had to be made to have the cabins fumigated to get rid of the smell before the aircraft could set off on the return journey.

WHISKY GALORE

While I was staying in Glasgow for the Scottish motor show at Kelvin Hall, I tried to pull off what I thought would be the best publicity stunt of the year. My plan was to run one of Rootes' latest trucks on Scotch whisky, but the result didn't turn out as I expected, although it did produce a good story and get publicity for us.

The trucks were powered by the remarkable TS3 engine which had been designed to run on any type of fuel, including paraffin, kerosine and even creosote. The engine was originally intended for military purposes and use in areas where there wasn't a regular supply of any one type of fuel, but it also proved to be an ideal engine for some of the smaller buses, because of its shape and size. Rootes further decided to use it as the power unit for a new medium range of trucks, which were being announced at the Scottish motor show.

As we were in Scotland, the home of Scotch whisky, I thought it would be a good idea to see whether it could be used as another fuel for our new truck. The engine's designers, however, couldn't tell me whether it would work. It evidently depended on the amount of water present in each bottle of whisky, but they thought it was an idea well worth trying.

John Melvin had been a friend of mine since my rallying days and his father owned Melvin Motors, in Glasgow, the main Rootes dealership there. As John's father was also that year's show President, I thought I would go to him for help. Several of John's friends owned distilleries and he not only agreed to obtain some cases of the higher proof export-only whisky from one of them, but also suggested that we should carry out the experiment at the main Melvin service station in the city.

I had one of the new trucks sent there, drained of all its diesel and fitted with a new fuel tank ready for the experiment, and when several cases of the finest export-only whisky arrived at my hotel, John and I set off with it for the Melvin service station.

We poured the contents of several bottles of whisky into the truck's fuel tank, to the obvious amazement of all the mechanics who stood around to watch. They must have thought we had gone mad as we poured some more whisky into the tank, but after several attempts to start the engine we gave up. Apart from a few encouraging splutters, the engine refused to start and it became obvious that the whisky wasn't going to work. We arranged for the truck to be collected later that day, put the remaining whisky in the boot of John's car and went back to the Midland Hotel for lunch.

It was mid-afternoon when we arrived at the show, but before we had even reached the Melvin Motors stand, John's father bounded across to meet us. He was obviously furious and wanted to know where his son had been.

"I've been with John Bullock," John replied, obviously surprised that his father seemed in such a state.

"And what were you doing?"

"We went to the service station to see whether we could run one of the new trucks on whisky."

"And what did you do with all the whisky?"

"We kept some for you," John said, thinking that his father was making sure that he didn't miss out on the special export whisky. "Don't worry, it's safely locked away in the boot of my car."

John's father looked as though he was going to have a fit:

"I'm not interested in that whisky," he bellowed. "What did you do with the whisky you were trying to run the engine with?"

"We left it in the fuel tank of the truck when we went to lunch."

"I know you did," John's father said, looking even more furious, if that were possible. "The mechanics drained the tank, drank all the whisky and are now drunk, every one of them. I've had to close the place down for the day because even the petrol pump attendants had been drinking the stuff and were giving petrol away to all our customers, with the compliments of Melvin Motors. It was lucky that I called in there after lunch, before the pumps ran dry."

John and I decided that discretion was the better part of valour and left his father to cool down. As we disappeared into the crowd he shouted after us:

"I hope you two don't have any more damn silly ideas planned for tomorrow!"

SCOTTISH IMPS AND CELEBRATIONS

The Scottish motoring writers were always very supportive of the Rootes Imp and the Linwood project. It was a shame that although it did eventually win many races and Rosemary Smith won the Tulip Rally outright in her Hillman Rallye Imp in 1965, it was a model which never managed to live up to expectations. The Linwood complex was finally closed down in 1981, after Peugeot had bought the old Rootes company from Chrysler.

The popular Rootes PR man in Scotland was the irrepressible Bill Morris, a wartime bomber pilot who had joined the company from the *Scottish Daily Record*. He nearly got off on the wrong foot on the day he arrived when Bill Garner, the Linwood Manufacturing Director, who was very proud of the improvements he had made to output since his arrival from Coventry, invited him to look round the factory before they had lunch together in the executives' dining room.

"Quite an impressive set-up, don't you think? Aren't you surprised at the number of different activities going on here?" Bill Garner asked the new arrival over lunch.

"I certainly am!" Bill Morris replied. "I'd no idea that Rootes made golf clubs for a start."

Bill Garner nearly had a fit. He was aware that the Scots were golf fanatics, but didn't know that a foremen in the aluminium foundry had hit on 'a nice little earner' and was making golf clubs there as a sideline.

Rootes had one of the finest pipe bands in Scotland, but without a doubt the smallest pipe major. He was not much over five feet tall, but a fine piper nonetheless. During a visit to the factory by Barbara Castle, the band played during lunch. As soon as she saw the television cameras arrive, much to everybody's amusement, she immediately walked up to an impressive looking six-foot piper at the front and congratulated him on the band's performance.

What she didn't realize was that she was talking to a raw recruit, who was only standing there so that the pipe major could hear if he played any wrong notes. The band's real pipe major stood by fuming, while the red-faced recruit received all the praise and attention from the Minister. There is no doubt she lost the Labour Party one supporter in Scotland that day.

Because of his height, our pipe major was the only one on Burns Night who could pipe in the haggis on the Garrick, a delightful old ship moored in Glasgow harbour, which had very little headroom below deck but was nevertheless a very popular venue for lunches and dinners. Bill Morris was also in great demand on Burns Nights, because of his ability to address the haggis. The only problem was that he never liked to let people down and was sometimes committed to attending several functions each year. He was naturally required to toast the haggis with a dram or two on each occasion and by the end of the evening had probably drunk the best part of a bottle of whisky. He usually got home safely, except on one occasion when he fell down and broke his arm, but even then insisted that it was due to a slippery pavement.

Bill Morris enjoyed telling the story of the motor industry guest who, after a good Burns dinner, decided to take a short cut back to his hotel through a cemetery. He fell down a newly dug grave in the dark and, unable to climb out, sat their shivering with cold. Eventually he heard footsteps and called out:

"Help! I'm freezing with the cold."

Another Burns Night reveller appeared, took a long hard look at the man shivering below, shook his head and said:

"It's nay wonder you're cold, you fool. You've kicked all your earth off!"

The Scottish Motoring Writers Guild used the Garrick for their annual dinner, which was always regarded as one of the best parties of the year. Guest invitations were much sought after and I always looked forward to the occasion. So did motoring personalities like Jim Clark and Jackie Stewart. The Garrick was moored in tidal waters, which meant that negotiating the steep gangplank, when the tide was out, needed a considerable amount of dexterity – no easy feat after an evening of true Scottish hospitality.

The Chrysler President told me on one occasion that he had an ambition to play some of Scotland's finest golf courses. I thought it would be a pleasant surprise if we arranged for him to do so during his next visit, and Bill Morris made use of all his friends and contacts in the golf world to line up some games for him.

The President was delighted and Bill was on hand at the first to introduce him to the Club Secretary and professional, who also had an experienced caddie standing by for their important American guest. Bill nearly fainted when the President went round to the boot of his car, took out a single club, put several different screw-on heads into a plastic bag and handed them to the caddie.

I never asked Bill to arrange a round of golf for anyone again.

A LAST WISH

When Gregor Grant was editor of *Autosport* magazine he was still a regular competitor in international rallies and could always be relied upon to keep everyone amused, particularly when he was with John Bolster, his friend and colleague for many years.

Any motor show, new model launch or race meeting was also bound to be enlivened by their presence. The only exception was before the start of one Monte Carlo Rally, when Gregor Grant was sitting in Fred Payne's bar, that popular watering hole in Paris, and suddenly became rather morbid.

"I don't like the thought of dying," he told John Bolster, who had been

trying to cheer him up. "When I do die, will you do me one last friendly act? To help me on my way will you promise to sprinkle the contents of one last bottle of good Scotch whisky over my grave?"

"You can rely on me, Gregor," John Bolster replied, "but as a good Scot I'm sure you won't mind if I drink it first."

A CLASSIC STYLE OF MOTORING

There was something rather weird about one of the main attractions at the 1995 *Retromobile* in Paris, acknowledged to be Europe's most prestigious classic car show, which attracts millions of pounds worth of almost priceless motoring gems. The name 'Helicar' rather gave the game away, along with the large propeller at the front, a flimsy plywood, fuselage-type body and its overall appearance which resembled an early-style aircraft without wings.

At various times since the turn of the century, there have been eccentrics who have tried to develop a flying car, but the French inventor Marcel Leyat was different. He wanted to produce a car without wings which would have the freedom of the air, but no gears, clutch or tyre wear. Leyat called his design the Helicar and built about 30 of them during the Twenties.

They were all two-seaters, with open or closed bodies, and they created tremendous interest, particularly when two were bought by a chocolate manufacturer and their drivers cavorted with them up and down the *Champs Elysees*, pirouetting between the other cars almost in their own length. Marcel Leyat took only 12 hours to drive one from Paris to Bordeaux in 1921 and a Helicar sped along the famous Montlhery circuit at close on 100mph.

When Roger Smith saw one at the Le Mans museum in the Eighties he decided to build a replica using as many as possible of the parts which its inventor would have used. He found a small 1,200cc flat-twin ABC engine, the right springs, a front axle and steering wheel, an old domestic switch for the magneto and a similar type of hand-throttle.

The Helicar didn't have any instruments and was steered through the rear wheels by a couple of thin wires going forward from the ends of the axle inside the body and then winding round the steering column. When the

steering wheel was turned, one wire shortened and the other lengthened to move the rear wheels in the direction the driver wished to go. The propeller was encased in a large wire mesh guard, for safety reasons, and the starting procedure was similar to that used for old aircraft. Once the Helicar started it was wise to have someone hold on to it to stop it from moving forward.

There was no reverse, but as the vehicle was light enough to be pushed with ease or lifted up at the back and moved about without difficulty, that didn't seem to be a problem. Both pedals were connected to the brakes, which could be operated individually, enabling the car to pivot when required. The driver's view forward was limited by the propeller, but the passenger was worse off, seated immediately behind the driver in a hammock-like seat.

Roger Smith has driven his creation at Vintage Sports Car Club events but has so far resisted Leyat's eventual modification: adding some wings and turning his Helicar into an aircraft. Perhaps the most sensible idea he had!

A MINOR MOSQUITO PROBLEM?

Classic car enthusiasts come in many shapes and sizes and from many walks of life, but they all have one thing in common: they get more fun from the cars of the past than from the latest models designed for the discerning motorist. Many of the old cars they own are in better condition now than they were when they left the factory. The really fanatical classic car owners go on to become what can be described as Concours Grand Masters, the small band of men and women who continually strive for perfection and hope to own the perfect old car which is entirely without a blemish of any kind.

You don't have to be a multi-millionaire to be a member of that select band, but being so would certainly help when the car is one of the more exotic models with a six-figure price tag and an insatiable thirst. Keith Fletcher certainly qualifies. He is a multi-millionaire classic car enthusiast who is always striving for perfection, but his pride and joy is a humble 1949 Morris Minor which he bought in poor condition for £4,000. He then spent a further £12,000 and nine months restoring it until it was in pristine condition.

He must surely be the most remarkable Morris Minor owner since the model first appeared in the Forties. He has been known to spend more than

50 hours a week cleaning and polishing his Morris Minor Convertible HER 697, and despite his millions, it is a task he says he would not leave to anyone else, not because they may forget to polish the floor under the carpets and behind the door trim or the underside, but because cleaning and polishing his concours-winning Minor is all part of the fun of ownership.

After every outing in the car, he goes through his strict cleaning routine which includes removing the wheels and dismantling the brakes to clean any dust from the linings. Concours judges can be very pernickety and will take into account the stitching on the hood, the state of the pedal rubbers, the type of bolts used to secure the wings, the condition of the toolkit and even the amount of air in the tyres.

Despite all the months of careful restoration work lavished on his humble Morris Minor, his devotion to detail and the hours of cleaning, polishing and preparation procedures, which always take place before an important *Concours d'Elegance*, his best mark has been a frustrating 99%: "I probably lost the other mark because I'd missed a mosquito on the radiator that day," he quipped. In addition to everything else, competitors in classic car Concours events obviously need a strong sense of humour, but if anyone is to achieve the elusive perfect score for their car Keith Fletcher must surely be an odds-on favourite.

ROOF-TOP MOTORING

Motoring during the Twenties and early Thirties maintained a delightful air of expectancy; something interesting was always likely to happen during a journey, particularly at weekends when many more families were able to take to the road. William Morris with his Morris Minors and Herbert Austin and his remarkably cheap and reliable Austin Sevens had certainly opened up motoring to the masses. There was also a spirit of friendship between car owners, and anyone in trouble could be sure of a helping hand from passing motorists, who knew that they themselves might be in need of help on another occasion.

As a small boy riding in the dickey seat of my father's Morris Oxford, I was always hoping that something would happen round the next bend which would turn a cold and blowy 'outing' into an interesting 'event' to tell one's schoolfriends about the following Monday.

This was often the case. On one particularly blustery Saturday afternoon we drove round a bend on a steep hill and came across an Austin Seven saloon which had been blown off the road by the wind. It was resting on its roof with the wheels still spinning. Inside was a rather large man who was trying to climb out through the window but had become stuck. We stopped, and my father joined several other passing motorists who had rushed to help.

Austin Seven saloons were particularly susceptible to high winds in those days because of their height: Herbert Austin still seemed to be under the impression that a gentleman should be able to get into his cars wearing a top hat! His Austin Seven saloon consequently had a high square roof, with enough headroom to allow several undertakers to sit inside wearing their professional headgear if they so wished.

My father and the other motorists managed to push the man back inside and told him to hold on while they lifted the little Austin onto its side and then back onto its four wheels. Neither the driver nor the car seemed any the worse for the experience, and after thanking everyone for their help, the man started the engine and drove off down the road. Even without the assistance of modern crash-testing equipment, car makers like Herbert Austin knew how to build cars which were strong enough to withstand landing on their roofs if they got caught in a particularly strong gust of wind.

For many cars steep hills proved a problem. It was not unusual to see a car climbing a hill backwards because it wouldn't go up in first gear, and reverse

was that much lower. The early Austin Chummy had an additional problem though: its fuel system was gravity-fed, which caused fuel starvation on very steep hills, so that owners had to turn round and reverse up!

Even so, the little Austin Seven quickly caught the imagination of the motoring public and was so popular that it became the subject of many music hall jokes. A favourite with comedians was the story of the Austin Seven which had run out of petrol and was standing at side of the road. The owner of a Bentley stopped, took out a rope and offered to tow the Austin Seven to the nearest garage. When the driver explained that the Austin's brakes weren't very good, the Bentley owner told him to sound his horn and flash his lights if they were going too fast and he would slow down.

Everything went well for the first few miles, until they were passed by a Lagonda and the owner of the Bentley towing the Austin Seven decided to give chase. Their speeds increased until they were going flat-out, with the Austin Seven driver frantically flashing his lights and sounding his horn. A policeman, almost knocked off his bicycle, hurried to the nearest telephone box and called his Sergeant in the next village:

"Take a look down the road, Sergeant," he pleaded. "I've never seen anything like it. There is a Lagonda and a Bentley both doing more than a 100mph and some idiot in an Austin Seven, sounding his horn and flashing his lights trying to get past both of them!"

It is a remarkable coincidence that the Austin company should now be owned by BMW. For many years the German company built Austin Sevens under licence and sold them under the name Dixie.

ONLY BANK MONEY

There are hundreds of car clubs in Britain, but I only know of one where none of the members were allowed to drive and all the usual motoring activities were strictly forbidden. All types of rally and treasure hunt were definitely out, and when I received an invitation to give a talk to its members I understood why. The address on the letter said 'Maidstone Jail Motor Club' and although I thought at first that it must be for warders and other staff, I was left in no doubt when I rang the prison that the members were all inmates.

I had never seen the inside of one of Her Majesty's prisons before and my own curiosity was a great enough incentive to accept the invitation immediately, even when I heard that the club meetings were always held on Sunday afternoons. Shortly before 2.30pm I parked my car near the front entrance and rang the bell. As the prison door clanged shut behind me and one of the warders took me to meet the club Chairman and Secretary, who were waiting for me in the inner sanctum, even the knowledge that I was only going to be inside the prison for a few hours didn't dispel the feeling of gloom I had as we made our way along the dreary corridors.

The club Chairman was a quietly spoken man in his fifties, but the Secretary looked a typical wide boy and reminded me of a bomb site car dealer I met after the war. They were both dressed in prison garb and I tried to imagine them in civilian suits. Speaking to a car club behind locked doors, where all the members were dressed in drab grey boiler suits and had warders watching them to make sure they didn't escape, seemed rather macabre at first, but they turned out to be a cheery bunch and I couldn't have had a more attentive audience. I found out later that the Chairman was a former accountant, who had been caught fiddling his company's books, and the Secretary was, as I thought, a secondhand car dealer. It was, perhaps, understandable that the members had chosen a reformed bank robber as their Treasurer.

I spoke for about 45 minutes on car design and the way in which the ordinary motorist benefited from the experience manufacturers gained by entering their cars in races and international rallies. My audience listened intently as I warmed to the subject and spoke about the programme of rigorous testing my own company put every new model through before it went on sale to the public. When I had finished the Chairman asked if there were any questions.

A rather mild-looking individual who was sitting about three rows from the front stood up.

"Yes," he said. "I have a question. Does the Ford Motor Company test all its new models as rigorously?"

I assured him that they did, but wondered if there was any particular reason why he had asked the question.

"It's just that I bought a new Ford and it gave me nothing but trouble. I sold it a few months later for what I could get."

"I'm sorry to hear that", I replied. "You must have just been very unfortunate. I hope you didn't lose too much money."

He shrugged his shoulders. "Didn't matter really," he admitted. "It was only bank money."

His comment caused a considerable amount of laughter and a wry smile on the face of the warder standing a few feet away.

"Who was that?", I whispered to the Chairman, who also seemed very amused.

"His main occupation was robbing banks and he was very good at it until he got caught and ended up here," he explained.

For the next half an hour or so I was faced with a barrage of questions about the motor industry, some of which I had difficulty in answering. There was certainly no shortage of knowledge about cars and car makers among members of that car club and they were obviously enjoying themselves, thinking up questions which they thought might stump me. I looked at my watch and realized the time had come when I could make my escape.

"I've exceeded my time and mustn't keep you any longer," I said with a feeling of relief as I sat down.

"You're not keeping me," came a voice from the back, "I've still got another six years to do!"

One of the prisoners in the main body of hall stood up and made an eloquent vote of thanks and, judging by the cheers as I got up to go, I must have made a reasonable job of answering their questions. When I was having tea with the Governor a few minutes later, I expressed surprise at how knowledgeable everybody had been about the motor industry.

"Oh, you shouldn't feel surprised", he said with a smile, "many of the people in your audience were from the motor industry."

I was rather flattered when I received another invitation to speak to members of the Maidstone Jail Car Club the following year, but remembered the remark made by the man who said he still had six years to do. I wondered how many more members were in a similar situation, and wrote to ask if this time I could talk about rallies and bring some films to illustrate the various points I wanted to make. I also offered to bring a projector and someone to work it. A reply came back that the films would be a great idea. The prison already had a projector and one of the club members had been a projectionist.

Apart from the rally films, I thought that I would enliven my talk with a cartoon I had seen which portrayed different types of car driver. I remembered in particular the exploits of a Mercedes owner, who behaved rather like Mr Toad in *Wind in the Willows*, and used his car's bonnet mascot as a gun-sight to target pedestrians and other road users. I asked our film librarian to get me a copy, but when I returned to my office late on Friday to collect the films, there was a note to say that the cartoon wasn't available but that another humorous short had been included which should be very suitable for the occasion. I put the films into the boot of my car and drove home quite looking forward to my second visit to Maidstone Jail, that weekend.

It was the same club Chairman and he introduced me to the projectionist, who made a note of the order in which I wanted the films shown, ending up with the funny. Everything went well, and as my talk ended I explained that I had one final film for them to see, which I hoped they would all enjoy. The lights went down and I relaxed to watch the funny, until I realized it was an extract from *The Great Train Robbery* showing a general free-for-all by a rebellious bunch of prisoners.

My film librarian with the warped sense of humour was right. The audience showed their approval by clapping, whistling and stamping their feet and shouts of "Go on, let him have it mate", but the reaction from the warders was somewhat different. If looks could kill I would never have left the room alive and as the film came to an end and the lights went up, there were calls from the warders to "Settle down now lads, you've had your bit of fun."

This time when I left the hall there was an even bigger cheer from the club members, but perhaps not surprisingly there was no invitation to have tea with the Governor. It was also the last occasion that I was asked to speak to a prison car club.

THE CROSS-EYED TOREADOR

Whenever a new model launch takes place in Spain it is a fair bet that there will be at least one photographer who will want to take shots of the car in a bullring with a toreador. This happened to Renault, and having got permission to use the local bullring, a leading French picture agency asked the company if it could provide a toreador for a photographic session planned for the following day.

However, employing a bullfighter at short notice, even in Spain, proved much more difficult than expected and the company's PR men were about to admit defeat when the local Renault dealer suggested Luis: "He is a

140

part-time toreador you are employing as a car washer to keep the press cars clean" they were told.

Their hopes were dashed somewhat when Luis turned out to be little more than four feet tall and had a very bad squint – hardly the image they had of a dashing toreador, even if he only did the job part-time at the local bullring. To make matters worse, because he was short of money he had hired out his *habit de lumiere* to someone else.

Even so, Luis was by then their only hope. The bullring had been booked and the photographic session with the agency had to go ahead. The little cross-eyed bullfighter was despatched with a pocket full of pesetas to reclaim his toreador's suit, get spruced up and be ready to be photographed the following morning in all his finery.

The agency photographer did his best, but try as he may, the close-up shots of a cross-eyed toreador posing in a bullring alongside a gleaming new Renault just didn't look right. In the end the only photographs which did appear in the French magazines showed the little bullfighter's back view, with the soapbox he was standing on hidden by his cape. What tough luck to have found the only cross-eyed, four-foot bullfighter in Spain!

A QUESTION OF PRIORITIES

The task of road-testing a new car in a foreign country can be enjoyable, but at times dangerous, particularly when a journalist has to share the driving with someone who may lack the necessary experience and ability to handle a powerful car safely at speed under unfamiliar conditions: on one occasion a car crashed into a ravine during a test drive when the driver used both hands to light his pipe and tried to steer with his elbows.

Most motoring writers seem to have nerves of steel and take the risks as a matter of course, but when an accident does happen, a good PR team knows what to do and goes quickly into action to ensure the injured driver's stay in hospital is made as comfortable as possible. There have been occasions, however, when their efforts to do so have had rather unexpected results....

That was the case when a leading British motoring writer was seriously injured in Spain. He lost control of the car he was driving because he was going too fast and it plunged down the side of a mountain, ending upside down on its roof. His passenger fortunately escaped with just a few cuts and bruises, but had the seat torn out of his trousers – to reveal a very bruised and red bottom. His colleagues immediately nicknamed him 'the baboon', because of the colour of his posterior and the way he walked until the swelling went down, which seemed to annoy him more than the crash.

The badly injured driver was rushed by ambulance to the American Hospital in Madrid and the company arranged for his wife to be flown from England to be at his bedside. No expense was spared. She was flown out First Class, booked into the best hotel and had a car and driver put at her disposal to enable her to visit her husband whenever she pleased.

When the company's PR chief met her at the airport it was evident that she had taken full advantage of the free champagne during the flight and seemed in no hurry to visit her husband. She booked into her hotel and then asked to be taken to a restaurant she had been told about, which served excellent lobsters and had a very good wine list. It also happened to be the most expensive eating place in town.

The PR man thought at first that her strange behaviour might be due to the shock of hearing about her husband's accident and that she didn't want to face up to the fact that he was lying seriously ill in hospital. However, that

theory was quickly dismissed the following morning when she announced that instead of visiting her husband, she had made an appointment to have her hair done and then planned to do some shopping. She also admitted that she had forgotten to bring her husband's spare set of false teeth to replace those damaged in the crash.

"There is nothing I can do about it now. He'll just have to eat bananas until the dentist can mend his others," she insisted. "He likes bananas."

By the end of the week it was quite obvious that all was not well with the marriage and that while her husband remained in hospital she planned to take full advantage of her free trip to Spain. There was little the car company could do about the situation except pay the bills and hope that she would eventually get tired of Madrid and lobsters and return to England before their PR budget ran out.

Fortunately, her husband made better progress than expected and within a few weeks was well enough to be flown home to England with his rather disgruntled wife, who had to accept that her free Spanish holiday had finally come to an end. Her husband not only survived the crash, but made a good recovery, which is more than could be said of their marriage.

A SALES DRIVE WITH
A DIFFERENCE

Car companies spend millions of pounds on market research each year, trying to find out who buys their cars and why. Yet for some time Rootes were at a loss to know why so many women living in the West End of London suddenly began buying the more expensive left-hand-drive Sunbeam models, which were usually difficult to sell in Britain; they simply refused to consider any models which had the steering on the right.

It was important to find out why, because during the Fifties and Sixties Rootes had a surfeit of low-mileage left-hand-drive models which had been bought new by visitors from overseas and members of the American forces stationed in Europe. The company then bought them back at an agreed price if their owners decided not to keep them when the time arrived for them to return home.

This 'buy back' scheme was Lord Rootes' idea. It not only enabled the company to earn millions of additional dollars at a time when he was Chairman of the Government's Dollar Exports Council, but also meant that visitors to Britain were able to have their own car, which they could take to the Continent with them if they wanted, instead of paying expensive hire charges.

The problem was that the scheme was such a success that Rootes were landed with many hundreds of left-hand-drive cars which people in Britain didn't want to buy, and converting them all to right-hand drive was far too expensive. We were consequently puzzled when the salesmen at the company's main London showrooms in Piccadilly suddenly had a sales bonanza, with left-hand-drive models in demand by women prepared to pay cash.

It remained a mystery until I came out of the Ritz Hotel in Piccadilly after lunch one day and was waiting to cross the road to Devonshire House. I noticed a smart left-hand-drive Sunbeam Rapier coming towards me, with an attractive young woman at the wheel. She slowed down to a crawl, wound down the window and invited me to join her. It was suddenly clear that Rootes' new left-hand-drive customers were prostitutes who were now finding curb crawling more profitable, less tiring and much safer than standing on street corners. They were also less likely to attract the attention of the police, who were cracking down on prostitution in London at the time and on street walkers in particular.

I watched the Rapier as its owner drove off in the direction of Park Lane, slowing down to talk to several men on the way. No wonder the company's new customers could afford to pay cash and buy the more expensive models: a left-hand-drive car gave them greater safety and must also have increased their earning power quite considerably. Having the steering on the left-hand side meant that they could talk to potential customers without having to lean across or stop.

When I told Peter Warrilow, the Rootes Sales Manager, who his new women customers were, he asked the obvious question. Here was a new source of income, but how could he advertise the fact and reach potential new customers? The only answer I could suggest was to place an

advertisement alongside those in London's Shepherd Market advertising 'French Lessons'.

Publicity is the life blood of sales and getting exposure for a company's cars on television can have an immediate effect, but not always for the good of a car's image, as I found out when the comedian Eric Barker asked whether I could supply a new Hillman Minx convertible for his new television series. We had just spent some time together in Coventry, where he had done the cabaret for us at a dealer convention we had held there, and his dry sense of humour had gone down very well with our guests. We'd had dinner with the Goons the previous evening and I was feeling in a good mood as we drove back to London.

Eric suddenly said, "I'd like to use a Hillman Minx convertible in my television show next week, but the only one we have belongs to my wife Pearl. It's not in very good condition and doesn't really do the model justice. Is there any chance of borrowing a new one?"

I was pleased to help and arranged for a white Hillman Minx press demonstrator to be delivered to the television studios at Shepherds Bush on the day of the show. I made sure it was spick and span and ready to show potential customers what a smart and attractive car it really was. I sent notes to Lord Rootes, his brother Sir Reginald and other senior executives of the company suggesting that they may like to tune in to the Eric Barker Show that evening. I even told some of our main dealers in case they might be interested.

The Hillman appeared in the first sketch and certainly achieved maximum exposure, but had I known what was about to happen I wouldn't have had the car within a hundred miles of the television studios, and I certainly wouldn't have encouraged any of my colleagues to watch the show.

The sketch featured Eric Barker as the owner of a brand-new car who was showing it off to his jealous neighbours, but when he tried to do so everything went wrong. Apart from refusing to start, it seemed to have every fault under the sun: the boot wouldn't open, and when he raised the bonnet there was a loud bang followed by smoke. It was Buster Keaton and Norman Wisdom rolled into one.

The situation went from bad to worse and I couldn't wait for the sketch to finish. Then the telephone calls began from colleagues, dealers and even Hillman owners who had been watching. I had my leg pulled unmercifully and it was fortunate that Lord Rootes and his brother saw the funny side of my gaffe, but gaffe it certainly was. I never arranged for another car to appear in a television show without first seeing the script. I didn't use Eric Barker again either!

BARGING ABOUT

A French inventor named Roussier designed a barge in 1907 which could be powered by a car, enabling it to cross a stretch of water, like a lake or loch, under its own steam if there wasn't a bridge, or if the normal ferry wasn't running. He thought it would be of particular value in the Scottish Highlands, where the lochs can be long, wide and deep and tourists can be faced with lengthy car journeys when they want to get to the other side.

His idea was quite simple: the barge would have either paddle wheels or a rear propeller operated by a pair of rollers at the stern. The car would be driven on until its rear wheels sank between the rollers and chocks were put in place to hold the front wheels. With the car in gear the engine and transmission spun the rear wheels and also the rollers, propelling the barge across the water.

There were, of course, pitfalls, one of which was that the driver had to make sure that he slowed the engine down in time before the barge reached the other side, otherwise it could easily become embedded in the opposite bank, scattering everyone in its path.

SUNK
ALMOST WITHOUT TRACE

Cars first started taking to the water in 1926 when Peugeot designed a motorboat car, built on a standard car chassis and powered by a 1.6-litre engine; it caused quite a stir at that year's French boat show. Six years later the German inventor Hans Trippel started making his Trippelwagen amphibious vehicles and testing them on the Rhine.

The Trippel SK6, which he introduced in 1937, had a 2-litre Adler engine, driving either the front wheels or a three-blade propeller, which gave it a top speed of more than 80mph on land and 12mph on water. It was later produced at Bugatti's Molsheim factory and he went on to produce the SG7, which had four-wheel drive and an air-cooled Tatra V8 engine at the rear.

Hans Trippel's Eurocar, powered by an Austin A35 engine, raised more than a few eyebrows when it was launched at the Geneva motor show in 1959, but from 1961 it was marketed as an Amphicar, and fitted with a 1,147cc Triumph Herald engine mounted behind the rear driving wheels. It was only capable of about 7mph on water and 65mph on land, which might have been one of the reasons why the wildly optimistic target of 20,000 was never reached and only about 800 were built.

Although it went out of production in 1963, several more were assembled from the large stocks of spare parts being stored at the German factory. The company eventually went bust in 1967 after spending more than a million pounds on research, and each employee was given one of the remaining Amphicars in place of severence pay. That is probably the reason why there are still so many of them in the Berlin area.

There are also 27 Amphicars in Britain and a flourishing fan club, as well as rumours of several more being hidden away in a barn somewhere in Leicestershire, put there years ago by a canny speculator. Optional extras for the later models included a pair of extension pipes which could be fitted to a bilge pump. One went into the water and the other could be fixed over the driver's head – to provide him with a shower after he had been swimming!

Although Amphicars usually stick to rivers and lakes when they take to the water, some have crossed the English Channel and one was run down by a

ship in the Straights of Dover. Like so many hundreds of other Amphicars, it was reported to have been sunk without trace!

CAN WE HAVE OUR WHEELS BACK?

Although the RAC Rally doesn't enable competitors to visit particularly exotic places, like some of the Continental events, it does pass through some magnificent scenery and can be a lot of fun for drivers, officials and spectators. It can be even more fun if one is driving a police car, as Norman Garrad and I found out on one occasion.

Rootes had entered a particularly strong Sunbeam team that year, with several Grand Prix drivers joining the regulars like Peter Harper and Sheila Van Damm. Norman Garrad, the Rootes Competitions Manager, and I decided to drive round the route together in one of the practice cars, so that we could keep up with the daily progress of the rally. During the drive down from Scotland our car suddenly developed gearbox trouble and when we reached Coventry we decided to call in at the Ryton-on-Dunsmore factory to change it over with a car from the sales demonstration fleet, while the Sunbeam was repaired.

149

However, it was the weekend and the demonstrators were all out on loan. Nevertheless, we found the keys for a Humber Super Snipe, which had been fully fitted out as a police car, complete with police signs, flashing lights and a siren.

It was Hobson's choice and we decided to take the Humber, rather than miss the next section of the rally, but we didn't realize the effect our change of cars would have on the behaviour of the competitors in the rally, particularly at night. They all started slowing down as soon as they saw us and we borrowed a couple of chauffeur's peaked caps so that we looked the part.

Rally cars queued up behind us, rather than accelerate past and risk exceeding the speed limit. When we put the police sign on at night the effect was even more dramatic and the sight of us parked in a side street was enough to keep everybody's speed down for several miles, in case there might be another police car further ahead.

The Rootes team knew what was going on, but it didn't take long for the news to spread round the other rally competitors. They still had to be careful not to mistake a genuine police car for us; "We thought it was those people from Rootes in their police car", would hardly have been an acceptable excuse if they had been caught speeding, and there was a general feeling of relief when our Sunbeam had been repaired and we handed back the police demonstrator.

My favourite international rally has always been the Alpine, particularly the build-up period the week before the start, when the Rootes team gathered at *La Reserve*. This was a delightful little *auberge* on the Mediterranean coast at Bandol, in the south of France, where the swimming, food and wine were all superb. The idea was to get everyone relaxed and in the right frame of mind before the rally got under way. The team cars and spares were taken there by transporter and the mechanics joined us to carry out last-minute adjustments to the cars and to join in the fun.

We took over *La Reserve* each year and had Bandol more or less to ourselves, apart from the local residents, until the peace and tranquility was broken one year by the arrival from England of the Triumph team, who had heard about our quiet haven and booked into a hotel a mile or so along the coast. They decided to liven up the proceedings one evening by raiding the bedrooms of our women drivers while we were having dinner, and taking away several items of their underwear as trophies. We didn't realize what had happened until the following morning when the women complained about their missing underwear. When we drove along the coast a little later, passing the hotel where the Triumph team were staying, we saw an assortment of bras and knickers flying from the flagpole in the grounds.

150

Most of the women took it in good part, but for some reason Norman Garrad wasn't particularly amused and neither was Sheila Van Damm, whose underwear had pride of place at the top of the flagpole. The women's honour was at stake, and fortified by several bottles of rather potent Bandol rose, a Rootes raiding party was organized to visit the Triumph team's hotel that night, where all their rally cars were lined up – as sitting targets. Each car was jacked up on blocks and had its wheels removed. These were then put in our transporter and driven off to a safe hiding place.

There was evidently panic when members of the Triumph team came down to breakfast the following morning to find all their cars without wheels. A deputation arrived at *La Reserve* while we were having breakfast to see if we were willing to declare a truce and return their wheels. We agreed, on condition that that we should be left in peace in future to enjoy the delights of Bandol and our *auberge*.

Stirling Moss was a member of the Rootes team most years and had a brilliant record in the rally, so much so that the organizers presented him with a special gold cup to mark his continuous run of successes at the wheel of a Sunbeam-Talbot.

Although the Alpine was probably the favourite international rally for most

competitors, the Corsican Rally was always a very friendly affair and produced some amusing incidents. On one occasion one of the rally cars went off the road at a particularly tricky bend and rolled down a steep bank before coming to rest in a deep ditch. As they did so there was a loud thud and the driver called out to his companion: "Are you all right?" A voice above replied, "Yes thank you, and how very kind of you to ask."

Another competitor's car, following close behind, had also come off the road and rolled down the bank at exactly the same spot, landing upside down on the car below.

Perhaps in today's politically correct society, with the two cars one on top of the other, he should have accused the first driver of "taking my space".

HOW MADAME LECOT GOT HER REGULAR SUPPLY OF NOUGAT

One of the greatest entrepreneurs in the history of the motor car was the Frenchman Andre Citroen, whose imaginative publicity stunts kept his products in the public eye before the war, but failed to stop his company from being sold to Michelin, when he finally ran out of money. The cause of his ultimate downfall was the revolutionary Citroen Traction Avant, a car far ahead of its time, with front-wheel drive and a chassis and body built in one piece, but it was very costly to produce and still had several faults when it was launched in May 1934.

Citroen badly needed a publicity coup which would create public acceptance and prove the car's reliability. So, with the help of his old friend Francois Lecot, he devised his last great stunt – by far the longest and most difficult to achieve. Francois Lecot was a well-known test driver and a veteran of many trials and rallies, who had already completed a 100,000-mile marathon in a Rosengart. Citroen now challenged him to drive 250,000 miles in less than a year in the new Traction Avant, but to do so would mean covering more than 600 miles a day, along busy roads, through towns and villages, averaging 40mph and spending 19 hours a day at the wheel.

Even so, it was a challenge Lecot readily accepted. He was bored with running their small family hotel at Rochetaillee and set about planning his attempt with military precision. As Rochetaillee was mid-way between Paris and Monte Carlo, he was able to alternate his route, so that he could drive to and from the *Place de la Concorde* in Paris one day and then head for the coast and Monte Carlo the next.

His plans were almost complete when Andre Citroen broke the news that he would have to pull out. The cost of overcoming the faults in the Traction Avant and producing the revolutionary new model had escalated to such an extent that he was facing bankruptcy and creditors were queuing up outside the factory each day demanding their money. The latest publicity stunt had been a desperate attempt to save the company, but Andre's health was failing rapidly and he was dying of cancer.

Despite the news, Francois Lecot decided to carry on and prove that such a feat was possible. Two skilled mechanics moved into the family hotel, along with the three scrutineers from the *Automobile Club de France*, whose task it was to oversee each journey. He left Rochetaillee at daybreak on July 23, 1935, accompanied by one of the *Automobile Club* scrutineers, and for the next 12 months Madame Lecot rose each morning at 4am to prepare coffee for her husband and that day's scrutineer, and to prepare a meal for the two mechanics who had worked all night on the black Citroen, making sure that it was ready for the daily journey to Paris or Monte Carlo.

Each evening, when the car arrived back at the hotel, the mechanics set to work making any repairs or adjustments Francois thought necessary, while he had dinner with his wife and grabbed a few hours' sleep before setting off again at daybreak, accompanied by a different scrutineer.

The Citroen was a standard production model, except that the windscreen hinged open to allow better visibility in foggy weather, and it had twin horns and headlights with coloured lenses to identify it to other road users. Lecot's exploits achieved a tremendous amount of publicity and the beret-clad figure and his black Citroen became a familiar sight during his daily dash to Paris or Monte Carlo. Well-wishers began lining the route to cheer him on and every time he passed through Montelimar, Francois always remembered to stop and buy his wife some of her favourite nougat.

Despite being off the road for several days when the Citroen hit a lorry, Francois completed the 250,000 miles on schedule, creating a record which has never been broken. The Traction Avant went on to form the basis of the Citroen range for more than 20 years, but despite his remarkable feat, Lecot failed in his attempt to join the army when the Second World War started: the authorities didn't consider him fit enough to be an army driver!

THE BATTLE OF THE 2CVs

The amazing Citroen 2CV has now been turned into a successful, although rather unlikely, racing car by a group of enthusiasts who organize an annual 24-hour Le Mans-type race for 2CVs at the Mondello Park racing circuit, to the west of Dublin. According to David Byers, the Racing Director, the first event for the remarkable little car much loved by students and conservationists was planned with the help of a bottle of Cointreau. Pints of Guinness are also much in evidence at Ireland's version of Le Mans, which now attracts entries from as far afield as America.

The 27 little 2CVs which lined up for the 1995 race were a sight to be remembered, along with the remarkable noise they made as the pace car turned off into the pit lane at the completion of the two warming-up laps. Their 'hotted-up' engines sounded as though they were blowing angry raspberries at the spectators when their enthusiastic drivers opened up the throttle with a dazzling display of foot-hard-down bravado.

There was plenty of bumping and boring at the end of the straight, with cars crashing into each other, and several had to make early visits to the pits for running repairs. When the race was first run, track-rod ends only lasted for about 10 laps, and some of the cars used up as many as four different engines. Because of this, several teams had as many as six spare engines in the pits for the 1995 race, as well as several gearboxes, just in case.

Pit stops are rather more casual affairs during the Mondello Park 24-hour event, compared with the highly professional activity which takes place when cars come in for repairs or refuelling at Le Mans – they have to be when the refuelling is done from jerry cans with the aid of a funnel!

Some of the cars were used for shopping and as everyday runabouts until a few days before the race, while others had been specially prepared to make them lower and lighter, and were fitted with stronger springs and shock absorbers.

A mauve and white car, which was one of the favourites, belongs to the rock band keyboard player Mike Lindup. He also owns a Ferrari Dino, but has been a 2CV race enthusiast since 1992. Another was entered by a team from the Japanese Nissan factory in Sunderland. A French girl working as an interpreter at the plant sold the car to them for £50, rather than going to the trouble of shipping it home to France. After a £500 rebuild it was ready to race.

The sponsors' names on a lime green 2CV with a number 9 painted on the side included 'John Stoker – joiner to the stars' and 'Auntie Elsie'. Number 19, painted a bright orange colour, was being driven by Eugene O'Brien, who only two weeks earlier had finished eighth at Le Mans in a Corvette.

As the race progressed, car number 13, entered by a Stoke-on-Trent team, took the lead, followed by car 24 from Glasgow, which wisely had a stalk light fixed to its roof as darkness fell so that it could be picked out more easily by the pit crew.

Several private battles developed as midnight approached and car number 11, an Irish entry, was seen parked not far from the bar with a notice on the windscreen which said 'Merely resting. Back in a few hours'!

By 2am, car number 13 was still in the lead, driven by Richard Dalton who, in a fit of enthusiasm, had shaved a Citroen chevron into his hair. A long line of deckchairs appeared as if by magic along the pit lane, their occupants shrouded in blankets, trying to grab a few hours' sleep while their colleagues tucked into fruit cake and coffee.

After 650 laps the fog became so dense and conditions had deteriorated so badly that racing was declared to be too dangerous. Red flags were waved by the marshals and the race was stopped for 90 minutes to allow the fog to lift. By 7.30am it had cleared sufficiently for the race to continue, with car 13 still in the lead.

Several of the pits looked like a scene from the BBC's *Steptoe and Son* series, with spare parts and engines scattered all around the place. The car driven by Eugene O'Brien was already on its third engine and several other entries also had new engines and gearboxes.

When the chequered flag went out at the end of the 24 hours, the lemon

and lilac car from Stoke-on-Trent, with lucky 13 on its side, crackled to a halt having lost its exhaust, after covering a very creditable 940 laps. It had managed to remain ahead of car number 24, the Glasgow entry, which finished in second place, and was the Stoke-on-Trent team's second successive win.

Welcome trays of Guinness appeared as the race scrutineers checked the leading cars, and miniature 2CVs in Dublin crystal were presented to the winners. Then the serious business of celebrating began, the like of which Le Mans has never seen!

BASIL FAWLTY MOTORISTS

The John Cleese character Basil Fawlty in the popular BBC series *Fawlty Towers* wasn't the first motorist to chastise his temperamental car. Neither was he the last. Basil Fawlty flew into a rage and beat his car with a branch, but as far back as 1903 a competitor in the Gordon Bennett race was far more pugnacious.

Spectators and officials had to leap for safety when L P Moers, the firm's chief engineer, drove his Peerless at full speed through the Athy Control. When the car ground to a halt a few miles later with engine trouble, he leapt out and threw stones at the radiator with such force that several of them penetrated the protective wire gauze, making a large hole, which put him out of the race.

More than 90 years later Craig Lambert lost his temper when the secondhand F-registered Ford Sierra, for which he had just paid £1,600, came to a halt because of a faulty fuel gauge. The rear-view mirror also kept on falling off, but the last straw came when he couldn't get to the shopping he had just bought. The 23-year-old builder got a loaded shotgun and fired seven shots into the side of the car, tearing holes in the rear passenger door, denting the wheelarch and ripping the upholstery and seats to shreds. Then he left it where it was and went off to watch television.

The police in Gloucester, fearing that a siege was in process, sealed off the street. They charged the frustrated motorist with criminal damage, intent to endanger life and possessing a loaded shotgun in public. Fortunately for him the magistrates saw the funny side of the situation and dropped the charges when he explained that the car had got the better of him and he wanted to take his revenge on it for the personal misery it had caused.

IN A CLASS OF ITS OWN

It must be the world's fastest, noisiest and most impractical saloon car, but even so, Renault consider their Espace Fl four-door, two-seater to be a phenomenally successful new model and well worth all the cost, thought and effort which went into designing and building it. From the start the company announced that it had no plans to market its new 187mph car and had built it purely for promotional purposes, to celebrate the first 10 years of standard Espace production by their partner Matra.

It is certainly in a class of its own. What other car is powered by an 800bhp Formula One engine taking up the space where the rear passengers would normally sit – particularly the engine from the Williams Grand Prix car which enabled Alain Prost to win the 1993 World Championship? How many cars can also go from a standstill to 124mph in 6.9 seconds, brake from 187mph to 44mph in only 80 metres, or drink a gallon of fuel every 4.3 miles?

A ride in the Espace F1 is certainly not for the faint-hearted, or for those who are unprepared for the experience and don't want to do themselves an injury. Apart from the noise of the 3.5-litre Renault V10 engine being loud enough to wake the dead, it can also cause ears to bleed if the occupants don't wear ear plugs.

There is little doubt that the Espace Fl is really more a projectile than a saloon car and needs a race track to show off its paces. Fortunately for weekend motorists, it is one Renault model they are never likely to meet on the roads when they are out for a leisurely drive, quite apart from the fact that it doesn't have an ignition key and needs an air starter to get it going.

When it has earned enough column-inches it will be retired to the company's museum, still considered to be a phenominally successful new model, without one having been sold. There can't be any other new model which can claim that achievement during the past 100 years!

A CAR LIKE THAT

The late Ted Ray, who was always a popular comedian at motor industry events, had a fund of good motoring anecdotes. A favourite was the story of the wealthy Texan farmer on holiday in England, who was driving down a narrow country lane in Devon when he came across a local farmer taking a heifer to market in a trailer drawn by an old tractor. The Texan stopped him and said:

"Say, will you tell me something? I've got 10,000 head of cattle in Texas, but I guess you do things differently over here. Would you mind telling me about your spread?"

The old Devon farmer took off his cap and scratched his head.

"Well sir, I wouldn't rightly call it a spread," he replied, knocking out his pipe on the tractor wheel, "more a sort of smallholding as you might say. To tell you the truth, I've got about 20 acres where I raise a few chickens and keep a cow or two. Then in the autumn I buy a few sheep because my missus likes a few lambs about the place come spring time."

The Texan farmer lit a big cigar and chuckled:

"Well now", he said, "isn't that just quaint. That just goes to show how differently we do things in Texas. Do you know, I can get in my car in the morning, be in my car all day and come night time I still haven't reached the other side of my farm."

"Fancy now," said the Devon farmer, "I had a car like that once and you've got my sympathy."

Hasn't everybody?